web design for ROI

Learn More ▶▶

Turning Browsers into Buyers & Prospects into Leads

Lance Loveday & Sandra Niehaus

Foreword by Kelly Goto

New Riders

VOICES THAT MATTER™

web design for ROI

Turning Browsers into Buyers & Prospects into Leads

Lance Loveday & Sandra Niehaus

New Riders | VOICES THAT MATTER™

Web Design for ROI: Turning Browsers into Buyers & Prospects into Leads

Lance Loveday and Sandra Niehaus

New Riders
1249 Eighth Street
Berkeley, CA 94710
510/524-2178
510/524-2221 (fax)

Find us on the Web at: www.newriders.com

To report errors, please send a note to errata@peachpit.com

New Riders is an imprint of Peachpit, a division of Pearson Education

Project Editor Michael J. Nolan	**Art Director** Sandra Niehaus
Development and Copy Editor Deb Carlen	**Cover and Interior Designer** Blair O'Neil
Technical Editors John Evans Amy Greer	**Compositors** Sara Chapman Scott Olling
Proofreader Josh Bogin	**Illustrator** Roger Gilliam
Indexer Julie Bess	**Production Editor** Connie Jeung-Mills

ISBN 13: 978-0-321-48982-1

ISBN 10: 0-321-48982-9

9 8 7 6 5 4 3 2 1

Printed and bound in the United States of America

contents

Dedications

To Courtney,

who chased around a toddler by herself
and went to bed alone so many nights
when I worked on the book,
while also pregnant with twins—
and for seven months after they were born.

This book would've never happened
without your constant love and support.

While being an author is the fulfillment of a lifelong dream,
you will always be the best thing that ever happened to me.

~ Lance

To Jody Perry

Teacher,

champion,

peaceful warrior,

and the love of my life,

who has brought me so many years of joy.

~ Sandra

About the Authors

Lance Loveday

As founder and CEO of Closed Loop Marketing (CLM), Lance's primary goal is helping organizations rethink and revitalize their approach to online marketing. CLM provides results-focused consulting on the entire 'closed loop' of an effective online marketing campaign, from initial strategy development to execution to ROI analysis, and has earned high praise from Hewlett-Packard, Quicken Loans, Salesforce.com, and many others for engineering results for them.

Lance has never been one to take the typical path. In search of the perfect career, he explored the fields of law, economics, politics, and endurance sports before diving into the Internet space.

With a knack (and a passion) for making online marketing exciting and engaging for novice and expert alike, Lance is a frequent speaker at industry and business conferences across the U.S.

Lance, his wife Courtney, and their three children reside in northern California.

Sandra Niehaus

Sandra is the VP User Experience and Creative Director at Closed Loop Marketing. She has been noted for her singular ability to balance business goals with design and Internet technology requirements, and has contributed her expertise to projects for a wide range of companies, including WebEx, Hewlett-Packard, Allstate Insurance, and VeriSign.

Sandra's creative and scientifically inclined family fostered her early fascination with technology and the arts. Since discovering the joys of computer programming in high school, she has pursued ongoing studies in computer science, business, writing, and music. She received a Masters in music composition from the San Francisco Conservatory of Music.

She joined forces with Lance at Closed Loop Marketing in 2004 after nearly a decade as an independent designer and web consultant. She resides in northern California, where she surfs, writes, practices mixed martial arts, and thinks about stuff.

Acknowledgments

When we started this venture, we had a vague vision of creating the book over leisurely cups of coffee while vacationing at a quiet seaside retreat. Reality quickly intruded to dispel this delusion. To make it possible for us to write at all, it took a support team of family, friends, counselors, advisors, co-workers, cheerleaders, and coffee baristas. We would like to specifically and deeply thank our long-suffering families and loved ones for their care, support, belief, and strategic goading.

Also, special thanks goes out to our colleagues at Closed Loop Marketing—Amy Greer, John Evans, Roger Gilliam, Amy Konefal, and Laura Albright—who took on extra projects, provided valuable feedback, found needed references, and put up with the teapot tempests that swirled around them.

Thanks to the team at New Riders, especially Michael Nolan, Mimi Heft, Nancy Aldrich-Ruenzel, and Connie Jeung-Mills for helping us shape and create this book.

Special gratitude goes to our editor, Deb Carlen of Five Ideas, who with humor, brilliance, and deep understanding—along with much plain-spoken feedback—transformed two wayward writers into authors. Sandra is especially grateful to Deb for curing her of using the word "just." Deb, you are the Queen of Editors and we couldn't have done this without you.

We also wish to thank and honor our book designer extraordinaire, Blair O'Neil of O'Neil Design Group, who brought our vision for the book to life with his astonishing creativity, expertise, patience, and humor. Through the craziest of times, Blair never compromised even a 1/32" on quality or our goals for the book. Thanks for having our backs and making us look so good, Blair.

Thanks to our great clients, many of whom provided support, encouragement, patience, and good humor during this effort.

There are many other friends and colleagues, both past and present, without whose support we likely wouldn't be here. Thanks to Bryan Eisenberg, Jeff Hackett, Scott Hogrefe, Chad Carlock, Taryn Moller, Molly Holzschlag, Jim Heid, and the Web Design World/Web Builder 2.0 conference teams.

Special thanks to Kayden Kelly and the team from Blast Advanced Media for their support, for last-minute proofreading assistance and for tolerating the occasional hostile takeover of their printer.

Special thanks to Barbara Coll (aka the Webmama) for her support over the years. Had Barb never introduced Lance to Jim Heid as a speaker to consider for Web Design World, this book would've never happened.

Special thanks to Kelly Goto for agreeing to write a foreword for us—and especially for doing so with a six-week-old baby at home.

Finally, it's a little known fact that writing a book together will test the bounds of any relationship. The authors wish to thank each other for picking each other up when needed and crossing the finish line together on this project while remaining respected colleagues and trusted friends throughout.

foreword

It's been more than a dozen years since I designed my first major web site. Shockwave was big at the time, as were large graphic downloads on a 14.4 modem. People were patient back then; the medium itself was so new and exciting that people didn't mind the wait. For businesses, the focus was on just having a web site. We launched the first entertainment online store and declared success when 24 people entered, perused the site and left—without buying anything. A lot has changed since then.

Today's web sites must generate revenue and real results. Now the focus is on creating web sites that add value, perform with ease, and offer services that people truly want. They call this 'user centered' and getting there is no easy task. For companies who depend on their web site to generate actual dollars and leads, a multi-faceted approach is necessary. Launching a web site is no longer the goal. It's just the first step in strategic web development.

Enter *Web Design for ROI*. Many web consultants and companies shy away from the term "ROI" because they don't or can't truly measure outcomes. But not Lance and Sandra. Their answer is to focus on "conversion optimization" which combines search engine and e commerce strategies with usability and user-centered design best practices. There's no magic involved here. The secret is to deliver what your customers need, mind the details and use metrics to guide small, iterative changes to your site on an ongoing, proactive basis.

Done properly, this approach results in increased revenue and lead generation. Sound easy? After you read the book and try its no nonsense approach, you may think so.

My advice: Read, review, implement and measure. The results will be worthwhile.

Kelly Goto
September 2007

introduction

introduction

"A man begins cutting his wisdom teeth the first time he bites off more than he can chew."

— *Herb Caen*

This book is a child borne, like many others, of a cosmic combination of passion, frustration, experience, and luck.

Passion—we quite simply love what we do and care deeply about the results. We hope we're able to communicate this in our writing.

Frustration—it seems for every victory we gain with clients, for every improvement we see through to completion, there are more battles to fight. And the word about usable, business-focused web design isn't spreading quickly enough for us. We joke (mostly) about being "endlessly offended" by the overall state of web design.

Experience—our combined 22 years working in the web space have taught us a great deal about success and what works—and about humility and the importance of testing assumptions, even "expert" ones. This book is the result of an ongoing effort to correlate and articulate our expertise in a clear, simple way; what we do, why we do it, and what we think is most important.

Luck—the stars surely collided to instigate this book. First, Lance decided to create a new presentation about how small changes to a web page design could increase effectiveness and conversions. Next, an acquisitions editor from Peachpit Press happened to see Lance present at Web Design World Seattle in 2006 and offered him a book deal practically on the spot. And lastly, as soon as Lance signed the book deal, he and his wife discovered they were expecting twins. So Lance turned to his colleague Sandra, pointing out they'd successfully co-written many an analysis, and how different could writing an entire book possibly be... ?

What is this book about?

At a high level, everyone understands it's a good thing to convert a greater percentage of web site visitors into sales or leads, but there's not as much understanding of how a site's design can help achieve that goal.

Luckily, it isn't rocket science. You start by understanding how visitors use a site. What do they want to accomplish? What are their concerns? What causes them to hesitate and lose faith in your site? Where do they abandon? Answer those questions, and apply your learnings to improve the site so it's more intuitive and usable for visitors. Then measure the result and adjust tactics based on what you learn, refining constantly as you add to your knowledge.

This book is a strategic and practical guide to improving any organization's web site effectiveness. We think every company with a web site would benefit from greater cross-pollination among those responsible for the site's success.

Imagine, for example, the synergistic, profitable effect an organization will see when:

- Business leaders understand web design
- Web marketers understand usability
- Developers understand the needs of a site's audience
- Web designers understand business goals and strategy
- Everyone understands metrics

But while that utopian vision is the underlying philosophy of this book, we've done our best to make it practical as well. We provide facts, guidelines, and real world examples that illustrate what we mean. Our hope is the book inspires those involved with a web site's success to re-think their approach and try something new.

Who is this book for?

These days it takes a village of people to inspire, envision, create, and maintain a web site. This book is for everyone in that village. We've attempted to make the book useful and accessible to people with a range of experience levels.

Many of the examples are from e-commerce sites. But the principles in this book apply to all types of sites: e-commerce, lead generation, content/media, non-profit, educational, and others.

How this book is organized

We've divided the book into three major sections:

- **The Big Picture—Chapters 1-3:** The first three chapters are about strategic issues: Why web design is important to business, the business case for better web design, and principles for effective web site management.

- **Design Guidelines—Chapters 4-9:** The next chapters focus on tactics for six different web site areas. Each of these chapters outlines the role and importance of the site area covered, what visitors want from it, and specific, actionable guidelines for improving results.

- **Resources—Chapter 10:** The final chapter includes a resource list for further exploration. More may be found on the book companion site at www.WD4ROI.com.

We've attempted to emphasize good design examples more than bad ones where possible, as good examples are generally more instructive. Where we've used imperfect examples, our intent is not to poke fun at the site or in any way criticize the people behind it, but to assist in illustrating the point.

What this book is NOT (the inevitable disclaimers)

We've accepted the fact that no single book can cover everything related to business and web design, no matter how enthusiastic the authors.

- **This book is NOT a design how-to checklist.** Each guideline should be viewed through the lens of your unique organization and implemented as an experiment. We think the guidelines are likely to improve a site's performance, but only by testing will you know for certain whether a recommendation is right for your site.

- **This book is NOT an exhaustive web design treatise.** Because of practical limitations, we focus on page types and features commonly found on web sites, and the concepts and guidelines we've found most valuable. In other words, we focus on areas where you'll get the most bang for your buck, the most return on investment.

- **This book is NOT about Web 2.0.** Because most web sites haven't yet tapped the full potential of Web 1.0—much less Web 2.0—we don't talk about Ajax, user-generated content, social media, or any of the other 2.0 buzzwords. We don't mean to downplay the significance of these new trends, but there is plenty to address in the current state of web design.

Web design ain't easy

Designing web sites in pursuit of a clear purpose requires substantial forethought and high levels of creativity, especially with the constraints under which most web teams labor. It's hard work, and our hats are off to all of those who manage to do it well. Our goal is to help all readers improve their sites, get the most out of their efforts, and achieve their organizational goals.

Visit us at www.WD4ROI.com

Although a book must, at some point, be set into type and printed onto tangible pieces of paper—which can be annoyingly foreign to those of us who work online—a web site is a fresh, updatable resource. For this reason we created a companion site for this book at www.WD4ROI.com to provide new information, links to additional helpful resources, a way to contact us with comments and feedback, and dates and places of related events, including presentations or seminars.

www.WD4ROI.com

We hope you'll visit us there!

Lance Loveday
Sandra Niehaus
Fall 2007

"We had no idea that this would turn into a global and public infrastructure."

~ Vinton Cerf, widely known as a "founding father" of the internet

chapter 1

a novel concept

"No matter how much Bill Gates may claim otherwise, he missed the Internet, like a barreling freight train that he didn't hear or see coming."

— *Jim Clark, co-founder of Netscape*

- 43% of all retail sales are expected to be influenced by or made on the Internet by 2012.*

- 83% of businesses use the Internet to research and find potential vendors.**

- 75% of web users admit making judgments about the credibility of an organization based on the design of its web site.***

Why are these figures significant? Because they validate something that most of us know intuitively: web sites play a major role in determining whether someone ultimately transacts with a company.

One naturally assumes, then, that organizations would be laser-focused on ensuring their sites are designed to capitalize on this opportunity, thereby maximizing their *return on investment (ROI)*.

Return on investment (ROI):
The ratio of money gained or lost on an investment relative to the amount of money invested.

---

* Forrester: "The Web's Impact on In-Store Sales: US Cross-Channel Sales Forecast, 2006 to 2012" and U.S. Department of Commerce.

**Enquiro: "Business to Business Survey 2007."

***Fogg, B.J., Stanford Guidelines for Web Credibility. Persuasive Technology Lab. Stanford University, 2002 (revised November 2003).

Strangely, that's not the case. Our experience indicates very few sites are designed with ROI in mind, and most under-perform relative to their potential as a result. In fact, most organizations seem oblivious to the impact that web design has on their organizational performance.

Although the Internet and web sites are relatively new, this scenario of organizations missing the obvious is not.

The science of shopping: a brief history

Consider the experience of brick-and-mortar retailers. Until recently they gave little thought to the shopper experience, or how seemingly unrelated environmental factors might impact a buyer's propensity to purchase. Aisles were narrow, lighting was poor; signage, if present, was treated as an afterthought. The prevailing sentiment of the shop owners could thus be characterized:

> "If people are interested in what we have, they'll buy. The design of our store doesn't matter as long as the right products are on the floor."

At the time, this attitude was accepted as common sense. There was no reason to believe otherwise. But when researchers started to track and study retail shopping behavior, they found that environmental factors had a profound impact on sales. In many cases the changes required to fix problems were relatively minor: move clothing racks away from the entrance so people aren't jostled while stopping to peruse an item, place dog treats on lower shelves because children and elderly people are usually responsible for those purchases, and so on.*

In all of these situations, sales increased as a result of acting on the new information. These recommendations seem obvious today, but weren't readily embraced at the time because the science of shopping behavior was in its infancy. Running a store was difficult, and retailers had more important things to do.

Sound familiar?

Over time, a set of best practices for store design, layout and signage were developed. But it took some time for most retailers to internalize and act on

---

The anecdotes in this section are from Paco Underhill's excellent book "Why We Buy: The Science of Shopping." If you're interested in the psychology of shopping behavior, this book is the best.

this new information. Some initially dismissed it, some paid lip service but did nothing, and some dabbled. Others saw its obvious power and potential, and dove in with both feet. Those early adopters reaped the benefits of increased sales and likely gained share on competitors.

Although difficult to measure, the adoption curve of the new science of (offline) shopping by retailers was probably very similar to Geoffrey Moore's description of consumers' adoption rate of new technologies in his book "Crossing the Chasm."

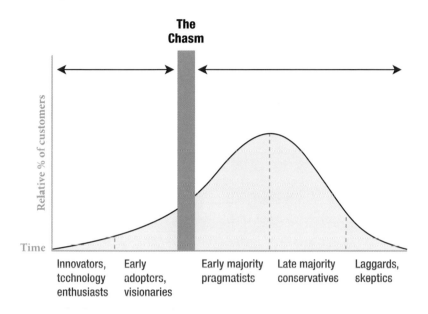

The Chasm

Relative % of customers

Time

| Innovators, technology enthusiasts | Early adopters, visionaries | Early majority pragmatists | Late majority conservatives | Laggards, skeptics |

The defining characteristic of this adoption model is the "chasm" which must be crossed before a new technology achieves mass adoption.

Today, major retailers acknowledge the power of store design to impact sales. They incorporate insights from research into the store planning and design process from the start. But the early adopters enjoyed a competitive advantage while waiting for rivals to cross the chasm.

What seems strange in retrospect is that it took so long for retailers to pay attention to store design. Doesn't it seem intuitive that providing a better shopping experience is good for sales? Not only will people linger longer and buy more, but they're more likely to have a positive impression of the store. And to relate their positive experience to friends, who will be predisposed toward shopping and buying at the store. So why *did* it take so long for merchants to start paying attention to store design?

What seems strange in restrospect is that it took so long for retailers to pay attention to store design. Doesn't it seem intuitive that providing a better shopping experience is good for sales?

Possibly because at the time they were focused on more traditional quantitative factors that they could measure and control. They simply couldn't envision how qualitative factors like store design could impact sales. Another explanation: they were so absorbed with internal machinations and company politics that they just didn't have time to think about the relationship between shopper experience and sales.

Moving online – and starting over

Following in the footsteps of their offline predecessors, the prevailing sentiment shared by many organizations about their web site is:

> "If people are interested in what we have, they'll buy. So long as we have all of our product and service information available somewhere, they'll find it."

Here we go again.

Of Economics and Web Design

Your web site: an investment

We argue that web sites should be viewed as investments, and that the decision process about web sites should be subject to the same level of discipline executives use when evaluating other types of investments. Business people decide to invest in an asset—an extra employee, a new manufacturing facility, or a sports team—based on whether the investment will yield a desired return on investment (ROI).

For example, say you're the CEO of a mid-sized manufacturing company. You have the opportunity to invest in some new software guaranteed to double the productivity of your workforce. A $1 million investment today will pay $3 million next year. To determine your ROI on the deal, divide the expected net gain by the amount of the initial investment and express the result as a percentage. Here's how to determine your net gain:

> *$3M return - $1M investment = $2M net gain*

To calculate ROI, you'd then divide the net gain by the amount of the initial investment:

> *$2M net gain / $1M investment = 2.00, or 200% ROI*

We argue web sites should be viewed as investments, and that the decision process about web sites should be subject to the same level of discipline executives use when evaluating other types of investments.

Assuming this is a guaranteed result (more on that in a second), this one's a no-brainer. You'd be ill-advised not to invest in something offering a guaranteed ROI of 200% in one year. Of course, it's not quite that simple: if it were, you would be buying islands, planning trips into space, and booking spa visits for your pets.

Choosing between investments

Most of us have limited dollars to invest. The same is true for businesses. The challenge for any responsible manager is choosing where to invest limited discretionary budget dollars to achieve the greatest return on their investments.

So how do they choose? Economists contend that a *rational person* will conduct an ROI analysis like that shown above for each activity, then select those that return the highest ROI until they run out of dollars. Continuing in your role as CEO, let's assume you have a $5 million budget and compile this list of investment options:

Rational person:

1) A person who always behaves in a logical manner.

2) A fictional economic construct useful for demonstrating economic theory, itself also largely fictional.

Investment	Cost	Return	ROI
New sales team	$1M	$2M	100%
Efficiency software	$1M	$3M	200%
Condo in Hawaii	$3M	$300,000	-90%
New brochures	$1M	$500,000	-50%
TV ad during Super Bowl	$2M	$400,000	-80%
Company health plan	$2M	$3M	150%
Company jet	$5M	$250,000	-95%
New web site	$1M	$4M	300%

The *rational* executive will reorder the possible investments by ROI so the list looks like this:

Investment	Cost	Return	ROI
New web site	$1M	$4M	300%
Efficiency software	$1M	$3M	200%
Company health plan	$2M	$3M	150%
New sales team	$1M	$2M	100%
New brochures	$1M	$500,000	-50%
TV ad during Super Bowl	$2M	$400,000	-80%
Condo in Hawaii	$3M	$300,000	-90%
Company jet	$5M	$250,000	-95%

… and then prioritize the investments that drive the highest ROI until the budget is used up. So the winners would be the web site, the efficiency software, the sales team and the company health plan. Easy, right?

Lies, damn lies, and economics

What's wrong with this picture?

- **We're assuming rational decisions.** As everyone knows, people are not always rational. It's part of our charm, and what makes us people. And most would agree that companies, especially large corporations, do not always act in a purely rational way.

- **Decisions aren't this simple.** It's rare that we have perfect information for decisions, and even the best analysis and most thorough due diligence can't predict the future with certainty. Then there's risk: investments with a high projected return or long time to payoff usually carry a high degree of risk, complicating decisions considerably. The result? Most organizations aren't willing to make decisions that risk losing money to pursue the potential big payoff associated with a long-odds bet.

- **The web site made the list.** Web sites are not usually considered a strategic asset worthy of serious investment.

Taking web design more seriously

The sad truth is that most organizations view their web sites and the people who design and build them as part of the "cost" in *cost center*. "No," they say, "the people at the tip of the spear who are generating revenue for the business are the salespeople." But how many people can even the best salesperson speak with in a given month? 50? 100? 200? While some reps may see an impressive number of people and influence how they view the company, a web designer's work may be viewed by millions of people every month, all of whom will make judgments about the organization based on their experience with the site. And research* has proven that visitors' ultimate likelihood to transact with an organization is heavily influenced by their experience with an organization's web site. The point is not to disparage salespeople, but to help prioritize the increasingly influential role that web design has in shaping how an organization is perceived.

Cost center:
Executive code for any obligatory support department that doesn't actually make money.

So why isn't web design taken more seriously?

Web Design is Broken: It's Probably Your Fault

We believe the way organizations *think* about web design is why so many web sites end up in the sorry state they do. If web design was valued as a way to expand profitability and achieve organizational objectives, we wouldn't see statistics like this:

*The average online shopping cart abandonment rate is 59.8%.***

That means only 4 in 10 people who put something into their shopping carts end up completing their transactions. This figure is dismaying, because we know that simple design changes usually result in a sizable drop in abandonment and *easy money* in the merchant's pocket. But most organizations don't even know what their abandonment rate is, or equally bad, accept a high abandonment rate as something they can't do much about.

Easy money:
Low-effort, low-risk, high-return investments. Normally rare. Prized for its ability to generate big profits.

* *Lindgaard G., Fernandes G. J., Dudek C. & Brown, J., "Attention web designers: You have 50 milliseconds to make a good first impression!" Behaviour and Information Technology, 25:115 - 126 (2006).*

** *Marketing Sherpa E-commerce Benchmark Guide.*

Given the low investment (basic design changes to make the cart and checkout process more intuitive) and high payoff (from 3% to 20% more revenue every month thereafter) you'd think online merchants would have made these changes already. But an *average* abandonment rate of 59.8% makes it clear that most organizations haven't even tried. Why?

Organizations end up getting in their own way and prioritizing poorly based on the most obviously visible elements (e.g., the home page) instead of those areas where changes may yield a higher ROI. We've worked on a lot of web design projects over the years, from projects for the smallest mom-and-pops to some of the largest Fortune 500 companies. Our experience convinces us that the way most web sites are managed, designed, and built is seriously flawed.

Blame management

"We need to have a picture of ducks on the home page because the CEO loves ducks."

Anyone who's been involved with web design for any length of time will recognize these common web design decision drivers:

- **Executive ego.** "We need to have a picture of ducks on the home page because the CEO loves ducks."

- **Competitor envy.** "Did you see the change Competicon, Inc. made to their site? We need to do the same exact thing. Now!"

- **Strategy by buzzword.** "We need to Ajax-ify our site and leverage Social Media to enable User-Generated Content. Everyone's going Web 2.0 and we can't afford to be left behind."

- **Tradition.** "That usability enhancement isn't consistent with our design standards."

All of which offers an unsettling and possibly controversial conclusion: Many people making the big decisions about web design today are unqualified to do so. How many CEOs and VPs of Marketing have a background in experience design, usability, or online marketing? How many of them could look at *and* understand their web analytics reports? How many of them actually observe as users interact with their site during user testing? Very few. Yet most don't think twice about making design decisions that have a huge impact on user experience.

To be clear, we're not advocating the removal of executives from the web design decision loop. We're advocating that executives collaborate with site managers and designers to make *better informed* decisions based on hard data, research, and web design best practices. Decisions that reflect an appreciation for the impact on the user experience and, accordingly, the site/business performance metrics. In other words, we think web design decisions deserve the same level of seriousness and discipline as other strategic business decisions.

We're making the case for treating web design as a critical role that has the same potential to impact an organization's success as Sales, Marketing, Legal, and Finance.

Blame IT

Because web design requires some technical skills, many organizations initially chose to place responsibility for their web site in the IT department, making the web marketing people dependent on IT to make site changes. The problem with this setup is that the IT group likely has multiple projects that take priority over the web site. So marketing-related requests end up at the bottom of the queue, and the web site rarely gets updated.

One of our clients has been trying for years to shift to a new content management platform only to be shot down by IT replying that her project was in *sustained engineering*, which has become one of our favorite euphemisms for "no," as in:

> "We're working on a major ERP installation right now, so we don't have the resources to tackle those web site changes. Ask the guys over in Sustained Engineering."

Blame designers

We don't let designers off the hook too easily, either. Many designers subjugate the user experience to their creative goals, ignoring the work's broader implications and instead treating the web site as an outlet for their creativity.

Others take a more technical approach, focusing on site technology instead of user experience and business impact. But does it help the organization to have a site with perfect XHTML and a poor user experience?

We're not advocating the removal of executives from the web design decision loop. We're advocating that executives collaborate with site managers and designers to make better informed decisions based on hard data, research and web design best practices.

Sustained engineering:
A euphemism used by technical people that means "We're never going to work on this project."

Web designers are in a unique position to play the role of user advocate, but to do so credibly requires designers to understand business language and inform themselves about goals, strategy, and metrics.

Blame the process

In fairness, the fault isn't all with executives, IT, *or* designers. Sometimes it's the web design *process* that's broken. Faced with an environment where they have limited control, people often control things they can change while ignoring things they can't.

Many organizations, particularly large ones, have a web development process that looks like this, with different specialists performing some work on the site before handing the project off to the next group.

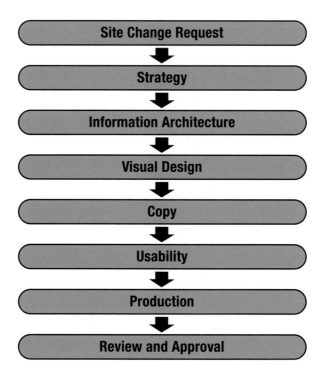

Like a giant game of "Telephone," the end result is often unrecognizable to the person initiating the request.

This arrangement offers the person making the request very little visibility during the process and therefore minimal influence over the end result. Each group makes dozens of subjective design and technology decisions based on their assumptions, interpretations, or personal preferences. Then, all those small decisions are incorporated into the final product in some way, but rarely communicated to the next group when the handoff occurs. So like a giant game of "Telephone," the end result is often unrecognizable to the person initiating the request.

To refine the process, many organizations develop additional guidelines, standards, and specifications. Such efforts are usually doomed: it's almost impossible to anticipate and account for each little decision comprising a web design project. And as we'll see later, it's those little decisions that make a big difference in the site's performance.

In recognition of the problems inherent in the traditional web development model, some progressive organizations are adopting the newer "agile development" model, which turns the old model on its head. The principles of agile development include: small teams, rapid iterations, constant refinement, and less documentation, among others.* We believe this model is the wave of the future, but very few organizations have yet to adopt it.

Blame the agency

> "That's a great idea, but we have an agency that does all our actual design work, so let's wait and see what they come up with."

Many organizations have outsourced the strategy, design and/or maintenance of web sites to an outside agency. We question the wisdom of outsourcing a function as fundamental as web strategy, as doing so can foster an unhealthy dependence on the agency. Yet this can work well where the agency truly understands the organization's strategies and target audiences, can successfully develop a site that melds the needs of both groups, and is held accountable for achieving specific business metrics. But it can also be a recipe for disaster if the agency is poorly managed, left in the dark about company strategy, or success metrics are never defined or enforced.

Sadly, there are also cases where the agency has a different agenda than the client. At the low end, we've seen "chop shop" agencies that prey on their less Internet-savvy clients and produce the same cookie-cutter sites for every client while charging for a custom design. At the high end, we've seen agencies who are more interested in winning awards and showcasing their creativity than in achieving their clients' objectives (if your agency uses the phrase "rich immersive experience" or similar terms to describe their goals for the site, you can relate to this scenario).

For an enjoyable and illuminating summary of the agile development approach to building web applications, we recommend reading "Getting Real" by 37signals.

Blame "old school" thinking

It isn't normal in most organizations for web designers to talk about business issues. It's so unexpected that it makes everyone uncomfortable when it happens. Executives roll their eyes at having to listen to some geek with no real-world experience ramble on about issues well beyond their job scope.

> "How can people who spend their days moving boxes around a computer screen know anything about running a successful business?"

Likewise, when executives start talking about design preferences, many designers treat them like children or respond in a passive-aggressive manner, certain that they lack the ability to appreciate the subtle nuances of design.

> "Sure, I can make the box blue instead of red. Of course that will ruin the design integrity of the page, so I'll have to redesign the whole thing. But now that I know you only care about the box being blue, I can probably do whatever I want with the rest of the page and you'll never notice."

Granted, these are extreme stereotypes. But this type of reaction is surprisingly common inside many organizations. And that drives us crazy, because we know that both ends of the spectrum are dead wrong. This kind of outdated thinking results in a lot of missed opportunities if the pattern doesn't change.

Blame "Internet time"

The web has only been a mainstream media vehicle for the past decade. As shown on the next page, its adoption curve has been steeper than any form of media to date.

Large organizations are notoriously slow movers. They aren't equipped to move as fast as the Internet requires to achieve online success. It's no surprise that they have been behind the curve in acting on the web's potential. The problem? Many organizations *still* treat the web as a buzzword although it's now become a critical communications vehicle.

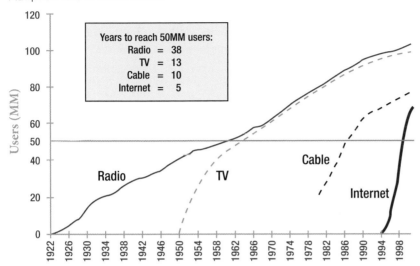

Adoption rate of mass media

Years to reach 50MM users:
Radio = 38
TV = 13
Cable = 10
Internet = 5

Sources: Morgan Stanley Technology Research: "E-Morgan Stanley Research Fstimate" and Harris Interactive: "Harris Poll #8." Data are for U.S. media adoption, using the launch of HBO in 1976 as the estimate for the beginning of cable as a mainstream media.

Breaking the cycle

While it's instructive (and amusing) to roast the sorry state of web design in most organizations, we simply want to make the case for a desperately needed new approach. If the leaders of these organizations truly believed in their web sites' strategic significance, they would address the problems. That they've allowed these problems to persist indicates a lack of seriousness about web design that may come back to haunt them.

You could get away with treating your web site like a pet project in 1998. But that attitude's a sure recipe for disaster now: the game has changed and the stakes have gone up.

You could get away with treating your web site like a pet project in 1998. But that attitude's a sure recipe for disaster now: the game has changed and the stakes have gone up.

You Have More Power Than You Think

You already have the power to enhance your web site performance by using design as a strategic weapon. In fact, if your site is like most of those we've worked with, you can probably gain an easy 10–50% lift in sales/leads just by implementing a handful of the guidelines in this book. While it may be tempting to dismiss this admittedly bold claim, there's substantial evidence to support it.

Jakob Nielsen of the Nielsen Norman Group (rightly considered one of the godfathers of web usability) published an article that estimated the following improvements based on a study of 42 usability-focused web redesign projects:

Metric	Average Improvement Across Web Projects
Sales / conversion rate	100%
Traffic / visitor count	150%
User performance / productivity	161%
Use of specific (target) features	202%

Source: http://www.useit.com/alertbox/20030107.html

Impressive gains are possible by enhancing usability, and many of the design guidelines in later chapters are grounded in usability principles. When usability is combined with a deep understanding of your audience and *conversion optimization* best practices, the results can be truly astronomical. Future Now, the largest conversion optimization consultancy, regularly reports gains in conversion and sales of over 300% for their clients.

Our experience aligns with these findings. We've seen gains of 30% to 1,000% as a result of focused conversion optimization initiatives. Estimating your own likely return will depend on many factors, of course, including your industry, objectives, online strategies, your site's quality, the target audience's expectations, and the competitive environment.

Conversion optimization:

The science and art of enhancing a web site's user experience with the goal of transforming the maximum number of visitors into customers.

Our goal isn't to convince you that a site redesign will double your sales. Our goal is to encourage you to think about how design can improve the user experience on your site and positively impact your business metrics. We hope you find our arguments and examples compelling enough to implement some of the specific design recommendations in the book. If you do an ROI analysis on the costs and benefits of making these changes, the decision should be simple. Making changes to your web site is relatively cheap and easy, while the potential payoff is comparatively high.

chapter 2

business case

"A guy don't walk on the lot lest he wants to buy. They're sitting out there waiting to give you their money. Are you gonna take it?"

— *Blake (Alec Baldwin), Glengarry Glen Ross*

Imagine you're a salesman trying to make quota. How would you go about getting more sales? There are really only two choices:

1. Make more sales calls

2. Convert more of the prospects you visit to sales (increase your *conversion rate*)

If you could only choose one of these options, where would you focus? If your goal is to get the most sales with the least effort, you'll opt to increase your conversion rate.

So why do we do the exact opposite with web sites?

Stuck in a rut

When confronted with the challenge of increasing online results, most organizations focus on option one by default: get more traffic to the site. More traffic yields a proportional gain in conversions (leads, sales, or whatever result you want from your site). To use the analogy of a sales funnel, the focus is on driving more people into the top of the funnel. More in equals more out. Problem solved.

But at what cost? There's the direct cost of purchasing more traffic, which limits the upside substantially, particularly in this age of ever-increasing

Conversion rate:
The percentage of unique visitors who take a desired action upon visiting a web site. The desired action may be submitting a sales lead, making a purchase, viewing a key page of the site, downloading a white paper, or some other measurable activity.

advertising costs. Then there's the *opportunity cost* to consider. Could the effort and expense of acquiring additional traffic have been better spent on an activity with a higher ROI?

What if that investment had instead been focused on increasing the site conversion rate, effectively widening the *bottom* of the online sales funnel? To validate whether to invest in buying more traffic or increasing conversion, we should conduct an ROI analysis on both options.

ROI Smackdown: More Traffic vs. Higher Conversion

Before we conduct the ROI analysis, let's gather some information to establish our baseline. The following examples are simplified to maximize clarity. Things are rarely this clear and easy. We encourage you to conduct a similar exercise using your site metrics, adjusting as needed for your situation.

Establish the baseline metrics

Say you have a site that currently has a 2% conversion rate, sales of $2M per month, and other baseline metrics shown below. To keep things simple, pretend we're selling an e-book so there are no product costs to calculate—only marketing (traffic) costs.

Monthly performance baseline

	Conversion Rate	Traffic	Conversions (Sales)	Average Revenue per Sale	Total Sales	Traffic Cost	Profit
Current	2%	1.0M	20,000	$100	$2.0M	$1.0M	$1.0M

Know your costs

What are the costs of the activities we are evaluating to improve on this performance? For this example, let's assume we have an extra $100K to invest in this business. We can either buy another $100K worth of traffic or spend $100K to attempt to increase our conversion rate. So the costs stack up like this:

Costs

Activity	Cost
More Traffic	$100K
Conversion Optimization	$100K

ROI analysis #1: buying more traffic

Now we have the basic information we need to project our potential return. If we assume that spending $100K on buying traffic will deliver 100K additional visitors then we can project our potential return on this activity as shown below:

ROI on buying more traffic

	Conversion Rate	Traffic	Conversions (Sales)	Average Revenue per Sale	Total Sales	ROI
Current	2%	1.0M	20,000	$100	$2.0M	—
Projected	2%	1.1M	22,000	$100	$2.2M	100%

So spending $100K on buying traffic will yield an additional $200K in sales and an ROI of 100%. That's pretty good. Now let's take a look at the ROI we could achieve by increasing our conversion rate.

ROI analysis #2: increasing conversion

Projecting the return on conversion is a bit trickier. To begin, we conduct a simple modeling exercise to measure the impact of any conversion rate increases.

It's difficult to forecast how much we can increase conversion, so we normally include a range of possible scenarios. To keep things simple, we've developed low, medium, and high conversion rate estimates of 2.1%, 2.5%, and 4% respectively. We then insert these estimated conversion rates into the chart to calculate the impact they have on sales and ROI.

ROI on increasing conversion

	Conversion Rate	Traffic	Conversions (Sales)	Average Revenue per Sale	Total Sales	ROI
Current	2%	1M	20,000	$100	$2.0M	—
Projections						
Low	2.1%	1M	21,000	$100	$2.1M	0%
Medium	2.5%	1M	25,000	$100	$2.5M	400%
High	4.0%	1M	40,000	$100	$4.0M	1,900%

In this simple example, there is a proportionate increase in sales for every increase in conversion rate; every 0.1% gain in conversion equates to another $100K in sales. If we assume our medium scenario is correct and we're able to increase the conversion rate from 2% to 2.5%, then sales will increase from $2M to $2.5M for a net sales increase of $500K, or an ROI of 400% on our $100K investment.

Nobody will believe this

What's that you're saying? It sounds too good to be true? OK. Although we know this type of conversion increase is within reach for most sites, we don't want to risk over-promising and under-delivering. So let's assume we can only attain our low estimate of 2.1%. That means we'd make an extra $100K in sales for our $100K investment, resulting in a *break-even ROI* of zero. So comparing the projected ROI on our investment options would look like this:

ROI analysis—1st month

Activity	Incremental Cost	Benefit – Month 1	ROI – Month 1
More Traffic	$100K	$200K	100%
Conversion Optimization— Low Estimate	$100K	$100K	0%

It doesn't look good for the conversion optimization project. But don't count it out. There's another factor we haven't accounted for yet: time.

Conversion optimization: the gift that keeps on giving

Remember that all of the information above is only for one month. That's the correct way to measure ROI for a variable cost pay-as-you-go activity like increasing traffic. Because buying traffic is a one-time cost with a one-time benefit. If you don't spend the same amount to buy traffic next month, you'll get less traffic and sales will decline accordingly.

But increasing your conversion rate is different. Increasing conversion is a one-time cost with an *ongoing* benefit. That means we'll make an extra $100K per month *every month thereafter* as a result of increasing conversion. So to accurately measure the return on increasing conversion one should measure ROI over a longer time period. Projecting ROI over the course of a year, we see these results:

Break-even ROI:

The point at which an opportunity returns only the amount invested.

Buying traffic is a one-time cost with a one-time benefit… Increasing conversion is a one-time cost with an ongoing benefit.

ROI analysis—1st year

Activity	Incremental Cost	Benefit Month 1	ROI Month 1	Benefit Annual	ROI Annual
More Traffic	$100K	$200K	100%	$200K	100%
Conversion Optimization— Low Estimate	$100K	$100K	0%	$1.2M	1,100%

Now instead of a one month ROI of zero we have an annual ROI of 1,100%! And that's for the low estimate, where we increased the conversion rate by only a tenth of a point—from 2% to 2.1%. That kind of gain is not difficult to achieve. As you'll recall, the average conversion lift from usability-focused redesigns was 100%, or double the baseline conversion rate. In this example, we're only raising the conversion rate by 5% (from 2% to 2.1%).

This analysis only covers one year, but the benefit of a higher conversion rate normally continues to accrue beyond that point. And most conversion optimization projects cost far less than $100K. The point we're making is that this is a conservative estimate of ROI on a conversion optimization project. In all likelihood, we'd achieve a higher conversion rate at a lower cost and yield the benefit over a longer period of time, any of which would increase the true ROI substantially.

That is the power of conversion optimization and web design for ROI.

So... when can we buy more traffic?

One could argue we'd be foolish not to also pursue the 100% ROI available from buying more traffic. We agree. But if you only have $100K to spend on one project or the other and conversion optimization is projected to deliver a higher ROI than buying more traffic, then conversion optimization should be prioritized first.

There is nothing stopping you from buying more traffic *after* you've optimized your conversion rate. In fact, that's exactly what we recommend. The upside of optimizing your conversion rate first is that you get the benefit of higher conversion for all future traffic. So the ROI on the traffic you buy will be even higher once you raise your conversion rate.

Think this doesn't apply to you?

Don't be so sure. Because ROI is expressed as a percentage, these numbers hold up whether you have actual sales of $200K, $2M or $20M. Regardless of your current sales volume and conversion rate, you almost always benefit from increasing the conversion rate on your site. But you can't make a fully informed decision if you never do the analysis.

The hard part of this analysis is accurately forecasting your return, which can vary widely depending on the estimated conversion rates you use. The process of generating the conversion rate scenarios to use in the initial model is more art than science, and it pays to be conservative with your estimates. The good news is that, as demonstrated above, you don't need to hit a home run and double the conversion rate to be successful. It usually requires only a very small gain in conversion to achieve a positive ROI.

Granted, we've kept things very simple in this analysis and omitted many assumptions, calculations and underlying data. But the principles are sound. And this type of analysis can be applied to any organization, whether the goal of the site is lead generation, sales, fundraising, recruiting, or anything else.

A different path

So there's our economic rationale underlying the argument for a new approach to web design. The numbers speak for themselves. However, most organizations don't think about their web sites in this way and probably never have conducted this type of analysis. They blindly follow the safe, well-worn path of buying more traffic. But because there are diminishing returns on buying more traffic, the time will come when they won't be able to buy more traffic *profitably*. At that point they will be forced to consider other ways to improve their online performance and may then finally focus on conversion. Meanwhile, organizations that already have optimized their conversion rates will have gained a competitive advantage.

It usually requires only a very small gain in conversion to achieve a positive ROI.

chapter 3

managing for ROI

"Here's an idea: The next time you're telling a story, have a POINT! It makes it so much more interesting for the listener!"

— *Neal Page (Steve Martin), Planes, Trains & Automobiles*

We're admittedly more annoyed than most by bad web design. But it isn't bad design itself that really bothers us. It's the missed opportunity to do something right. The wasted potential. And the wasted effort.

It takes as much or more time and money for companies to create poor designs—and thus poor user experiences—as it would take to create good designs and good user experiences. We hate seeing all that money being left on the table.

Our goal is to help you get the most from your web investment. To do so requires avoiding much of the dysfunction that plagues so many web projects. To help with this, we've compiled some key principles for successfully managing web sites for optimal ROI:

- **Know What You Want**
- **Know Your Audience**
- **Treat Your Web Site Like a Business**
- **Create a Web Site Strategy**
- **Measure the *Right* Metrics**
- **Prioritize Design Efforts Intelligently**
- **Test, Learn, Repeat**

Know What You Want

Pop quiz:

1. What are you trying to accomplish with your web site?

2. How satisfied are you with the design and usability of your site?

Many people hesitate before answering the first question, which concerns us. But *everyone* has an opinion about the design and usability of their current site. It surprises us how many people are quick to point out how dissatisfied they are with their web site. So while many organizations may not have a clear idea what they're trying to do with their site, they're pretty sure it isn't working.

Ask the right questions

The first question to ask about any web site:

"How can we use our site to achieve organizational objectives?"

Common answers:

- Increase sales
- Generate leads
- Reduce support costs
- Foster loyalty among customers
- Streamline processes with partners

The list of possible responses goes on, because ways to use the web increase daily and sites pursue many of these objectives simultaneously. But before an organization can start effectively brainstorming opportunities, someone needs to ask the question.

Because your web site is likely only one of many in your industry, another question to ask is:

"What opportunities are we missing because we have a poor or mediocre web site compared to our competition?"

The answers are similar to those above, and the addition of the competitive threat helps acknowledge that the success or failure of a web site is determined by customers, not by you. Framing the question this way also highlights the real cost associated with settling for a below average web site: the opportunity cost.

Know Your Audience

Who's this thing for?

Web sites should be designed for the audiences they're trying to reach. Yet many organizations make little attempt to anticipate likely visitor needs, much less design their sites to address them. Often, design decisions are based on bad (or badly outdated) assumptions. For example, many government sites have navigation options based on their organizational structure. This seems perfectly logical to the government employees, who know that building permits are issued by the Community Development department. But it's obviously a mistake to assume that the average person will make that association. What concerns us is the message that such designs send about what it's like to work with that organization.

Do you get it?

In contrast, the organizations that "get it" start by asking questions, like:

- Why are people coming to our site?
- What are they expecting to find?
- How can we make our site easier for them to use?

This involves thinking about the site from the visitor's perspective, which can be difficult. Human nature is tricky: once we learn something, it's hard to imagine not knowing it. This is why user testing can be so valuable; it reminds us that most people don't know what we know.

User testing: the secret weapon

User testing is an invaluable tool in developing real knowledge about audience behavior. It can help reduce the often strong influences that personal preferences and bad assumptions play in web design decisions. It can also help remove the subjectivity around interpreting whether a particular design is working or not. If 80% of users experience a problem that prevents them from taking the desired action, it's a pretty clear signal that something is wrong with the design.

This is why user testing can be so valuable; it reminds us that most people don't know what we know.

Everyone involved in web design should see a user test of actual web users. Seeing firsthand how people surf the web drives home how most of the debates about web design are about topics that ultimately don't matter. Debates about the thickness of the drop shadow on the navigation tend to fade in importance as soon as the team sees a prospect struggling to find the Add to Cart button.

User testing has traditionally been reserved for larger organizations with the budget to hire big agencies who rent special-purpose testing rooms with multiple cameras and one-way glass. But no more. Now you can buy some software* and a webcam, install it on a laptop, and presto! You have a mobile user testing lab able to record and synchronize the user's screen movements, their audio commentary, facial expressions, and other responses. You can embed time-stamped notes in the file during recording on another networked computer, then edit the whole file later to create highlight reels. The interface looks like this:

We think user testing is woefully underutilized, and advise everyone to conduct some form of it, either in-house or by hiring an agency. It's relatively inexpensive, easy, and often yields valuable insights that translate to an immediate increase in conversion and ROI.

*The user testing software we use is called Morae from TechSmith. We're big fans of TechSmith's other products as well. Check them out at www.techsmith.com.

Please note that user testing isn't for the faint of heart. It can be agonizing for designers and site managers to see people try and fail to use their creations. Years ago, we had one client, while observing a user struggle with his site from behind one-way glass, become so frustrated that he actually shouted "IT'S RIGHT THERE, DAMMIT!" so loudly that the participant heard him. The client got some coaching on user testing etiquette. The participant got to leave early.

Build your knowledge

Knowledge of your audience is both an input to and output of the approach we're advocating. We need a certain level of knowledge to be even minimally successful in designing a site. Because it is so valuable, we recommend acquiring as much audience knowledge as possible—before, during, and after any design project. This requires incorporating user testing and/or other forms of user feedback into the web design process. While this can add time and expense, it is a necessary step if optimal results are desired.

Developing knowledge of your audience so you can see your site through their eyes is the real power behind our approach. If there is a secret to our success, that's it.

It isn't about you. It's about the audience.

Please note that user testing isn't for the faint of heart. It can be agonizing for designers and site managers to see people try and fail to use their creations.

Treat Your Web Site Like a Business

"The web is changing the rules of business," says the hype. There may be some truth to that idea, but the basic rules of business still apply—especially the rule about needing a plan to get anywhere. To optimize web site investment, we believe every organization should document a web site strategy.

A web site strategy spells out the game plan for your site much the same way that a business plan sets forth key information about an organization's products, services, and strategic direction. But while a business plan focuses on the big idea behind a company and its market positioning, a web site strategy spells out how the site contributes to the larger business goals, and includes elements unique to the online space. Ideally, a business plan and a site strategy dovetail perfectly so it's clear how the site supports the broader goals of the business plan.

Web strategy vs. web documentation

There's generally no lack of web site documentation. Most larger organizations have some of the following: design guidelines, coding guidelines, site maps, accessibility guidelines, navigation standards, functional specifications, security standards: the list goes on. They usually don't, however, have the one document that truly informs and makes sense of all the others: a site strategy. The other documentation is still critically important, but the narrow, detailed focus of most web site documentation can lead to poor prioritization, resulting in more time spent producing perfect documentation than creating a better user experience. It's easy to lose focus on the goal while obsessing about accessibility standards or the myriad other things required to build a web site.

The absence of a site strategy is a critical omission. Put another way: if you don't know where you're going, it doesn't really matter which direction you choose. The moment you have a clear goal and communicate a well-defined web site strategy to the organization, everyone can rally around the cause and find ways to contribute.

Create a Web Site Strategy

We've included below the components we think every site strategy should contain. This is not a complete list—there are too many potentially successful strategies and variations of site plans for there to be only one "right" plan. Include these factors and others as appropriate for your unique situation.

The examples below are based on fictional company XYZ, which manufactures and sells water-saving irrigation equipment. See a completed site strategy document, as well as a blank template you can use, on our web site at www.WD4ROI.com.

Objectives

List the primary organizational objectives for the web site. Many people confuse objectives and strategies. The difference: objectives are goals; strategies are the means to achieve one or more objectives. Objectives explain *what* you are trying to accomplish while strategies explain *how* to accomplish them. Make your objectives specific and measurable, so you'll know when you achieve them.

> *Objectives explain what you are trying to accomplish while strategies explain how to accomplish them.*

Example:

Grow online sales by 25% over the next 12 months without an increase in ad spending.

Audiences

List all potential audiences you want your site to reach. We generally recommend breaking out primary (those from whom you expect to receive the greatest ROI) and secondary audiences (everyone else). This is a revealing exercise by itself, as it encourages those involved to acknowledge how many different types of people visit the site.

Example:

- **Primary Audience.** *Prospective customers.*
- **Secondary Audiences.** *Customers, potential investors, partners and potential partners, analysts/press, employees and potential employees.*

Primary audience profile

Include the characteristics of the primary target audience for your site. Are they senior citizens on a fixed income, IT executives at major corporations, or teenaged girls obsessed with Japanese animation? List everything you know about your primary audience: demographics, key decision drivers, what's appealing to them about your product or service, and anything else that offers insight into what makes them tick.

If your organization already has conducted customer profiling or segmentation studies, insert the results of that research here. More advanced organizations may have *personas* developed for this purpose. Personas can be an excellent way to get inside customers' heads and understand them better.

Personas:
Fictitious characters created to represent different user types. A persona description includes users' goals, concerns, and their likely questions.

> ***Example:***
>
> *Currently, XYZ's primary audience is comprised of two major groups. In order of priority, they are:*
>
> - ***Builders and Developers.*** *Companies who invest in, develop or remodel residential and commercial land and real estate. The target individuals in this group are decision makers and influencers for landscaping, budgeting, and liability issues. Their primary concerns are how our products can attain cost savings, regulatory relief, and credibility as a "green" builder.*
>
> - ***Homeowners.*** *Affluent homeowners in one of two subgroups: new homeowners planning to install new landscaping; and existing homeowners with 1/8 acre or more, with landscaping auto irrigation in place and monthly water use charges of $20 or more. Both groups place importance on water savings, price and convenience.*

Audience questions

Brainstorm a list of questions each audience member may have when visiting the site. Phrasing audience concerns in the form of questions is beneficial, as it helps the entire team to see the site from the target audience's perspective.

These questions can also serve as a helpful checklist later during the design review process. By evaluating designs to ensure each question is answered and that the path to the information is evident, you can easily uncover possible design flaws that might have otherwise gone undetected.

Example audience questions

Audience: All

General

- *What does XYZ do?*
- *How do the products and services work, exactly?*
- *How does using XYZ compare with what I'm doing now?*
- *What are some typical results for my type of situation?*
- *Are services available in my area?*
- *How much does the product/service cost?*

Credibility

- *Who are XYZ's customers? Are there any similar to me?*
- *What do customers say about the product/service?*

Next Steps

- *Are there any deals/special offers available?*
- *Can I talk to a live person?*
- *How do I get started?*
- *Do you have printable material I could show my spouse/boss/colleagues?*

Audience: Builders/Developers

- *Is the service easy enough for my employees to install and use?*
- *Will you be at any upcoming tradeshow/industry events?*
- *Do you offer any partnership opportunities or special pricing for my type of business?*

Audience: Homeowners

- *Is the service easy to install myself?*
- *Can I retrofit an existing system?*
- *Is the system easy to use?*

Competitive assessment

List three to five major competitors in this section and compare their web sites to yours. Pay special attention to competitors' *calls to action*—these can help you reverse-engineer their web site strategies. Be sure to include a good cross-section of the competition, paying special attention to companies with better web sites, regardless of their size. It's much better to benchmark against a tiny competitor who has a fantastic site than a large competitor who has a terrible site. We like to include screen shots of each company's home page and important secondary pages as well. Viewing these designs side-by-side offers significant insight into messaging strategies and can provide a glimpse into how different competitors have dealt with various design decisions.

> *Example:*
>
> *Competicon, Inc.*
> *At first glance, there is not a major, distinctive difference between Competicon and XYZ. Competicon appears very similar in messaging, general branding appearance, products, services, and benefits.*
>
> *Although not without its problems, the Competicon site is better organized and surfaces important benefits and information more quickly and clearly than XYZ's site. Competicon also appears more credible than XYZ with its inclusion of numerous industry and customer quotes site-wide, and detailed information on their key management team members and advisors. The cumulative effect creates the impression of a solid, highly regarded company.*
>
> *Calls to action: View Product Demo, Download White Paper.*

Traffic sources

Provide a brief summary about how the site will be marketed. Include any marketing activity you believe will result in traffic to the site. Provide a breakdown of the percentage of site traffic expected from each major source.

It's important to think through how and why people visit the site. These factors reveal a lot about visitor mindset and expectations, and the information helps you tweak the design to accommodate their needs from the start. It can also surface the need to create separate landing pages (discussed in the next chapter) for different audience types.

Call to action:
The action requested by a marketer's content; often the next step a consumer takes toward the purchase of a product or service. Examples include Buy Now, Add to Cart or Register for Newsletter.

Example:

Traffic Source	Percentage of Total Traffic
Paid search campaign	30%
Organic search	25%
E-mail campaign	25%
Direct navigation (typed or bookmarked URL)	10%
Partner sites	5%
Banner ad campaign	5%

Strategies

Finally, we get to strategies! Repeat your objectives here, and list the specific strategies that will be employed to achieve each objective.

Our placement of strategies here is by design. Why place strategies at the very end of what is ostensibly a strategy document? Because to develop optimally effective strategies, you need all the elements listed above firmly in mind.

Example:

Objective:
Grow online leads by 25% over the next 12 months without increasing online ad spending.

Strategies:

- *Enhance search engine optimization efforts to drive incremental free traffic.*

- *Refine paid search campaigns to drive higher volumes of qualified traffic at the same or lower cost-per-click (CPC).*

- *Redesign selected areas to increase conversion rate on direct, organic, and partner (non-campaign) traffic.*

- *Develop custom landing pages for each primary target audience and product to increase conversion rate on banner, e-mail, and paid search (campaign) traffic.*

Metrics

Detail the metrics that will measure the success of your objectives and strategies. It's critical to choose the right metrics to track.

> *Example:*
>
> - *Online lead volume (total, and by source)*
> - *Organic search referral volume*
> - *Paid search traffic volume*
> - *Conversion rate on non-campaign traffic*
> - *Conversion rate on campaign traffic*
> - *Cost/conversion for campaign traffic*
> - *Task completion rate and anecdotal feedback from quarterly user testing*

Measure the *Right* Metrics

How does your web site contribute measurably to your organization's objectives?

If your standard answer includes the word "hits" please take a moment to close this book and whack yourself in the head with it. There. Now remember that every time you're tempted to use the term again. It's an open secret in the web design community that anyone who uses the word "hits" in reference to their web site most likely has no idea what they are talking about. Just don't tell anyone we told you.

Problems with web reporting tools

As the web is still a relatively new and fast-changing medium, there are no commonly accepted standards for how to measure the success of a web site. Many organizations default to tracking the metrics most prominently displayed in their web analytics reporting systems. This is problematic for a number of reasons, among them:

- **Too much data, not enough intelligence.** One of the great things about the web is that it gives us the ability to measure so much. In fact, many organizations have built custom databases and dashboards to summarize the daily, monthly and weekly performance of their sites. We're huge proponents of developing dashboards, knowing your metrics and using them to track your success. But the easy availability of data often fosters over-reliance on it—to the point that the data is all many executives and site managers see or think about when considering their sites. And because they are fixated on the numbers, they have a hard time appreciating the more qualitative metrics that can be equally, if not more, valuable. Put simply, they make no attempt to understand the *why* behind the numbers.

- **They aren't perfect.** There have been multiple studies on how different web analytics packages provide different results for the same exact sites. Each one measures things just differently enough to ensure meaningful disparity between any two tracking systems. There also seems to be a certain amount of inexplicable "I've never seen that before" randomness in the results that one needs to accept when dealing with web reporting tools. When these problems surface, organizations lose confidence in the data. Some give up tracking entirely and some spend a lot of time and resources trying to troubleshoot the problems. Neither approach ends well.

- **They lack context.** Almost all analytics packages provide the same basic information by default: Visits, page views, time on site, returning visitors, and so on. The problem: that information by itself doesn't tell you anything. In the example below from Google Analytics (the best free tool on the market), we see there were 2,567 visits over the selected time period. Is that good? Bad? Average? Without digging deeper and performing some analysis, you just don't know. In fairness, the analytics providers have made great strides in enhancing the usability and usefulness of their tools in recent years. But most of them still emphasize the same metrics they always have.

We see there were 2,567 visits over the selected time period. Is that good? Bad? Average? Without digging deeper and performing some analysis, you just don't know.

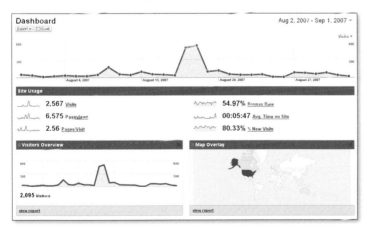

As a result of these problems, many organizations don't know which metrics they should be tracking, don't trust the metrics they do track, and/or don't know how to interpret that information to derive actionable intelligence.

Measuring web site success: key principles

Like so many other important tasks, measuring web site success is an art and a science unique to each organization. As with design, there are few hard and fast rules when it comes to the "right" way to measure web site success. But we have general principles we've developed in response to our experiences and observations about how most organizations deal with this topic.

- **Focus on what people *do*, not what they *say*.** It may seem counter-intuitive to some, but what people say in response to a questionnaire or focus group question often does not reflect what they really think. Likewise, asking people to tell you how they would behave in a given situation is not an accurate predictor of how they will actually behave in that scenario. If reality was a reflection of what people say, then the world would be full of good drivers with above average kids.

- **Follow the money.** The most valuable web metrics are those most closely related to the organization's success. And success metrics denominated in dollars tend to get more attention than any others. If you aren't able to track sales originating from the web site, at least develop a system that allows you to express the dollar value of the web site's contribution to the organization's success. It's much more compelling to say "Web sales were up $100K last month as a result of increasing our conversion rate" than "We increased our conversion rate by 0.1%."

- **Focus on trends, not snapshots.** Resist the temptation to obsess about short-term results. Yes, significant anomalies should be investigated and corrected if truly problematic. But it is counter-productive to focus too much on the inevitable short-term fluctuations in results.

- **Consistency beats accuracy.** Because web analytics data is rarely 100% accurate and trends are more important than point-in-time statistics, it's important to ensure that metrics are tracked consistently over a long period of time. Doing so ensures the validity of long-term trends and comparisons of results between two time periods.

- **Close the loop.** Be sure to integrate the web site with any sales force automation (SFA) or customer relationship management (CRM) systems you use. Most of those systems make it very easy to automatically import and manage data from web forms. Integrating these systems with your site gives you the powerful ability to track customer behavior from "click to close" and beyond.

If reality was a reflection of what people say, then the world would be full of good drivers with above average kids.

- **Triangulate with different types of metrics.** It is helpful to track different types of metrics from multiple sources. We advise tracking a combination of absolute (e.g., revenue) and relative (e.g., conversion rate), as well as quantitative and qualitative results. This is one way to enforce some checks and balances on the metrics that are tracked, as sudden spikes or drops in some metrics may be easily explained by activity in another area, thus minimizing the potential for panic and unnecessary fire drills. The ability to see how variations in one metric affect other metrics also enables a deeper understanding of underlying visitor behavior patterns, which can provide valuable intelligence.

The metrics that matter

The right metrics are usually a combination of business metrics, site metrics, and user metrics. We recommend regularly reporting on all three types of metrics in the same "dashboard" style report.

- **Business metrics.** These metrics are the same that the organization uses to measure success at a high level. They are usually pulled from a sales/lead management system or another critical business system used by the whole company.

- **Site metrics.** As explained above, web site metrics provide statistics on site usage. They're usually sourced from a web analytics reporting tool.

- **User metrics.** User metrics are derived from user feedback mechanisms, most commonly surveys, focus groups, and user testing. The most valuable user metrics usually come from user testing.

Examples of each type of metric

Business Metrics	Site Metrics	User Metrics
Revenue	Conversion rate	User testing results
Transactions	Most visited pages	Satisfaction survey trends
Profit	Time on site	Focus group feedback
Gross margin	Traffic	Customer support inquiries

Metrics examples for a few types of sites*

Site Type	Metrics
E-commerce sites	Revenue
	Profit
	Conversion rate
	Average order value
	Average cost per conversion
Lead generation sites	Lead volume
	Conversion rate
	Revenue originating from web leads
	Cost per lead
	Revenue per visit
Ad-based content sites	Revenue
	Profit
	Average page views per visit
	Average cost per visit
	Average revenue per visit

While important to track all of these metrics on a site-wide basis, it's also critical to break out these metrics by traffic source as well. Doing so can enable good insight into which campaigns are performing well and which may not be, so that marketing efforts and spending levels can be optimized for ROI.

* *For an excellent summary of web analytics, see "Web Analytics Demystified" from Eric Peterson. And for a more complete list of recommended metrics to track for various types of sites, see Eric's "Big Book of Key Performance Indicators." Both are available at http:// www.webanalyticsdemystified.com.*

Metrics that don't matter (as much)

As we've shared our view on the most critical metrics you should be tracking above, we also wanted to call out those we feel are less important and explain why.

- **Traffic.** This is probably the most common metric. However, focusing on total traffic as a success indicator by itself can be misleading because not all traffic is equally valuable. If you drive 100K additional visitors to your site but none of them becomes a customer, you haven't really accomplished anything. Using traffic as a measure of web site success would be like a brick-and-mortar shop owner measuring success by the number of people who stop to look at the window display. If an action doesn't contribute to making the cash register ring at some point, then it probably isn't worth tracking.

- **Time on site and average page views.** These can be good directional indicators, but are prone to misinterpretation. For example, if the average time on site decreases after a redesign, that isn't necessarily a bad thing. Especially if sales are up because it's easier to find and buy products.

- **Hits.** Hits simply measure the number of objects (text units, graphics, and other code elements) downloaded from a web site. The number of hits can be easily inflated merely by adding more pictures to your site. Fortunately most analytics vendors have de-emphasized this metric now. But there was a time when hits were the metric used to gauge a site's audience. In 1998 you could get venture capital funding for having a site with a million hits. Especially if it was losing money.

- **Surveys.** Surveys are particularly poor indicators of site success. First, the questions in many surveys are subjective and poorly worded, introducing some form of bias in the responses. Next, they are usually offered on an opt-in basis, meaning people can choose to take them or not. This skews survey responses toward those who have a strong emotional feeling (positive or negative) about the company or site, as those less motivated to provide feedback are likely to click No Thank You and move on. Attempting to encourage survey responses by using incentives only exacerbates the problem, as the results are then skewed toward those motivated by the free prize. Finally, the number of responses received for many surveys is not statistically significant, meaning any conclusions drawn from the results are prone to be incorrect. If you want to use surveys, we advise screening the questionnaire to remove potential bias and using the same exact survey over a long period of time to develop a trend.

If an action doesn't contribute to making the cash register ring at some point, then it probably isn't worth tracking.

- **Focus groups.** The problem with asking people questions in a focus group setting is that their answers are often colored by what they think you want to hear, societal norms, peer pressure, politeness, and other factors. We'll say it again: Pay more attention to what people *do* than what they *say*.

- **Industry average conversion rates.** The desire to benchmark one's performance against the competition is understandable. However, to enable a true apples-to-apples comparison of conversion rates between sites the audience expectations, traffic quality, call to action, offer, and more would have to be exactly the same. You would essentially need to have the same site as your competition for the comparison to be valid.

Prioritize Design Efforts Intelligently

Just as most organizations opt to buy more traffic rather than increase their conversion rates, they also focus the majority of their design attention on a single page. Can you guess which one?

If your organization is like most, the home page gets the most focus. Next are higher level index or category pages, followed by detail pages. Deeper pages like forms and checkout processes are an afterthought and get almost no attention. Landing pages, if they exist, are likewise below the radar. Generally the higher the page in the site hierarchy, the more attention it gets. So the level of design attention paid to various pages of the site looks like this for most organizations:

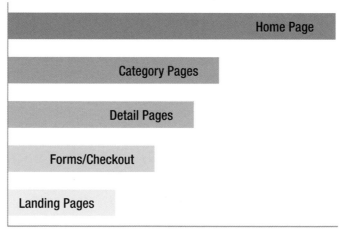

Design Attention

But if viewed from a potential ROI standpoint, it *might* look more like this:

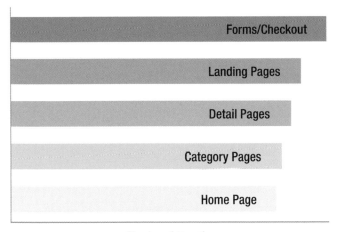

Design Attention

Obviously, it's more rational to prioritize design efforts according to projected ROI.

Use analytics to pinpoint problem areas

Web analytics tools can yield some valuable intelligence if configured and used properly. In addition to providing the type of "good" metrics discussed previously, they help identify problem areas on a site. This usually requires diving into the data or setting up custom reports, but it's really not that hard to do. The goal is to identify specific pages where visitors abandon the site or are sidetracked from taking the desired action. Those pages with high dropoff or abandon rates should be prioritized for design attention to assess whether there's an opportunity for improvement.

For an example of this process in action see the "Stop Reading and Try This" section at the end of Chapter 9.

Estimate ROI on design projects

When we've identified one or more pages with abnormally high dropoff rates, we can project the impact that redesigning the page for a lower dropoff rate will have on key metrics and overall ROI. It's easiest to conduct this type of analysis on a self-contained area of the site where visitors generally follow a predefined path, such as a multi-page application or shopping cart*. Again, it's helpful to model different scenarios and use conservative estimates.

If a conservative estimate indicates a substantial gain is available from redesigning the page, then it's probably worth the effort. Be sure to look for those "low-hanging fruit" opportunities: projects with a high projected ROI which require minimal effort.

Just as we used an ROI analysis to make the case for conversion enhancement efforts, we advocate conducting ROI analyses on every major web design initiative. Doing this provides a framework for decision-making that is objective and rational, thereby reducing the emotion, ego and politicking that seems to drive so many web design decisions. Viewing design efforts in this light also helps everyone think through the implications of their contributions to the bottom line, enabling them to prioritize their efforts. Finally, it establishes concrete and measurable goals for the entire team, which provides a level of accountability so often missing from design-related projects.

Test, Learn, Repeat

Are we done yet?

No. Web sites are never "done." Except for a few obvious exceptions, web sites should be viewed as long-term strategic initiatives. Technology is always changing, the competitive environment is changing and, most importantly, user expectations evolve. Web sites will always need updating to capitalize on the latest conditions; this is why we think of web sites as ongoing experiments rather than projects.

We use the term "experiment" purposely, as it is representative of the open-minded and scientific approach we advocate. There is a universe of potential design options available for any organization. The design guidelines and examples included later in this book will help improve your site's performance—perhaps dramatically. Incremental improvement is a worthy objective, but the ultimate goal is to achieve designs that produce optimal results for your organization.

....

* *We acknowledge that it is almost impossible to develop a foolproof mechanism for projecting ROI, as not all sales or leads are created equal. Additionally, there are normally multiple prospect actions with different values that can be tracked. For this reason, it's helpful to develop a scoring system that places custom values on different types of leads and actions.*

The potential upside for most organizations' web sites is tremendous. The common thread between those few organizations that come closest to realizing their potential is their zealous focus on testing. It pays to test.

Yes, it takes serious discipline to adopt this approach to web design and testing, but the benefits are substantial. If it were easy, everyone would be doing it.

Up Next

We've organized the rest of the book to cover common site sections:

- Landing pages
- Home pages
- Category pages
- Detail pages
- Forms
- Checkout processes

Your site's sections may have different names, of course. We went with this naming scheme to be as inclusive as possible.

Within each chapter, we take the ROI-focused approach to web design outlined thus far and apply it at a page-specific level, using these high level categories:

- Your goals
- Visitor goals/questions
- Key metrics
- Unique issues
- Design guidelines and examples

Bend or ignore the guidelines as appropriate to your situation. If a guideline doesn't speak to you, we hope you'll still gain some value from the thinking behind it, and an enhanced awareness of your audience overall.

Because we want to encourage readers to act on this information, we've also included a section called "Stop Reading and Try This" in each chapter. In this area we provide simple recommended actions to gain a better understanding of how visitors interact with your site.

The common thread between those few organizations that come closest to realizing their potential is their zealous focus on testing. It pays to test.

chapter 4

landing pages

"Sir, don't you think we should turn on the runway lights?"
"No, that's just what they're expecting us to do!"

— *Airplane*

In the good ol' days of the Web (a mere decade ago), forward-thinking companies had web sites. And that was it. When you wanted to link to your site, you chose one of your pages and linked to it. No big deal. You only had 15 pages on your site anyhow, and the number of "hits" was all that really mattered.

We like to think we've come a long way since then.

Today, forward-thinking companies realize it's not enough simply to drop marketing campaign traffic onto an existing page and hope for the best, especially when campaigns cost thousands or millions of dollars a month. These companies want their money's worth and more: They want to see traffic converting into leads and sales.

Enter the custom landing page. It's a web site's stand-in for ambassador, concierge, and superstar salesperson rolled into one. It's been carefully crafted to meet, assist, and convert visitors into customers. Most landing pages are specifically developed to support marketing campaigns, and this is the type of landing page we'll discuss in this chapter.

Landing pages are not a new concept, but their potential impact is still often overlooked. Whether you're a small company with a single product or a large company creating thousands of landing pages on the fly, making a few simple changes to the first page a visitor sees has an astounding impact.

The first step is to stop using generic web site pages as landing pages, and create a custom experience for visitors. Organizations taking this simple step report conversion increases ranging from a solid 10% to a mind-blowing 3,000%*. If you already use custom landing pages, then making some design and copy changes can further improve your results.

At this point, you may be wondering: "Come on, can changes to a landing page really have a such a dramatic impact?"

Yes, they can. It all starts with understanding your audience.

Visitor Questions

In Chapter 3 we recommended you anticipate all the possible questions your visitors may have when they arrive at your site. Since that's a pretty tall order, we provide a list for each page type to help get you started. Below are some typical questions visitors will have when they arrive on a landing page. If the answer to any of these questions is "No" or simply isn't available, it's unlikely the visitor will convert.

Will your visitor answer "No" to any of these questions?

- Is this what I expected to see?
- Does this look credible and trustworthy?
- Does this look interesting enough to spend more time here?

Will your visitor find the answers to these questions?

- Hmm… that's intriguing. How do I learn more?
- I'm interested, what now?
- What if I'm uncomfortable doing that?
- And if I have more questions?

Each product and service inspires its own specific questions from visitors, of course. This is where you come in: the better your understanding of your audience, the more accurate your list of questions.

Now that we have a better idea of what your visitors will want to know, let's take a look at what you want them to do.

Of course, the highest improvement rates are usually seen for pages so far out of whack there's no place to go but up.

Landing Page Goals

The goal of a landing page is to move the visitor to take the primary desired action. The selection of that action, whether it's a purchase, a newsletter subscription, or a brochure download, is a business decision driven by an online business strategy. For instance, if the business goal for a web site is lead generation, the landing page goal will be to motivate visitors to make contact or share their contact data. If the business goal is sales, the landing page goal will be to move the visitor forward in the sales cycle.

Since defining the right online strategy to achieve a business goal is a complex task beyond the scope of this book, we're going to assume you already know what you want your landing pages to accomplish. However, here are a few examples of specific landing page conversion goals and how they might map to a business goal:

The selection of the desired visitor action is a business decision, one that is driven by an online business strategy.

Business Goal	Landing Page Goal	Desired Visitor Action
Lead generation	Collect contact information from potential customers qualified by showing interest in a white paper topic	Visitor registers for a free white paper
Lead generation	Collect e-mail addresses to use as a marketing outreach for new products	Visitor requests free Tips Sheet via e-mail
E-commerce	Sell a product	Visitor clicks the Add to Cart button
Viral marketing	Spread the word about your organization, site, products, or services	Visitor sends link to a friend
Branding	Entertain visitors who in turn encourage more visitors, enabling higher sales of on-site advertising and eventual sale of company to Google	Visitor views a funny video

It's important to keep business goals firmly in mind while designing landing pages and thinking through the conversion process. If you have a clear vision of the desired result, the difficult design decisions and tradeoffs needed to achieve it are easier to make.

Key Metrics for Landing Pages

Once you've set your landing page goals, the next step is to determine whether the landing page effectively achieves those goals. Fortunately this is easy, because there's only one metric that matters for most landing pages:

- **Conversion Rate.** The percentage of visitors who successfully complete the primary desired action. Counting the number of visitors who reach a unique "success" or "thank you" page—one accessible only via the landing page—is the simplest way to determine this.

Example:

In July one specific landing page—Landing Page A—receives 1,000 unique visitors. During that same time period, 250 unique visitors arrive on Success Page A, the unique "success" page associated with Landing Page A. The landing page conversion rate is

$$250 / 1,000 = 25\%.$$

Considerations

- **Accurate tracking.** Many sites use the same "success" page for multiple landing pages, or use dynamic landing pages that have very similar URLs. This type of scenario increases the complexity of tracking conversions for each individual landing page, so make sure your analytics package provides sufficiently advanced tools.

- **The source of traffic.** Not all traffic is created equal, and some sources are more likely to send highly qualified prospects—those more likely to convert—than others. If you're able to track each referral source individually all the way to conversion, you'll have a better sense of the traffic quality different marketing venues and approaches provide.

- **The result.** Be sure to also look at the big picture by tracking from landing page through to the final goal. If 100% of landing page visitors download a free white paper but only 0.01% later convert into customers, there may be other issues unrelated to the conversion and sales process.

Unique Issues for Landing Pages

Landing pages have some unique issues requiring special attention to the overall focus, balance, and design of the page.

They must integrate the entire sales cycle

Landing pages are unique animals in the conversion zoo because they are tasked with independently performing the entire *sales cycle*. Even if visitors arrive already interested in an offer, the landing page must still attract and hold their attention to prevent them from leaving. If they stay, the page must create or reinforce interest, then instill desire, and finally guide the visitor to take action. That's a lot to ask of a single page!

They must perform quickly

One key difference between a landing page and its human counterparts (ambassador, concierge and salesperson) is time. Visitors are often hurrying and multi-tasking. This behavior allows the landing page a mere handful of seconds, not leisurely minutes or hours over coffee, to perform its numerous duties.

They have more first-time visitors

The percentage of first-time visitors to a landing pages is often higher compared to other areas of a site. Why? Because people may type in a URL to a home page or bookmark a product page to come back to later, but they almost always stumble across a landing page after clicking on an ad, often after performing a search. This type of visitor is probably less familiar with the company and has no particular reason to trust it at first.

Sales cycle:

A description of the steps in the sales process. One example is the AIDA Sales Cycle, which describes potential customers as progressing from Attention to Interest, to Desire, and finally to Action.

Landing Page Design Guidelines

So, how exactly do you whip the landing page into shape so it answers visitors' questions and meets business goals? Here are some effective guidelines to test on your site.

Establish credibility

As we mentioned earlier, it's vital that a landing page represent a company well since they're often the first contact with a visitor. A successful ambassador or salesperson will arrive with excellent references and present a sparkling, well-dressed appearance. A landing page can do the same through design, function, and visible references.

Use a professional, industry-appropriate design

A landing page provides visitors with a first, often subconscious, impression about a company. Employing a design that's inappropriate for an industry, or that's noticeably less professional than competitors, does little to increase visitor confidence in the quality of a product or service. And that initial impression can spread like a virus, infecting perception of the rest of the site.

Take a look at the sites of competitors and other authoritative sites within your industry. Include product review sites, industry-specific news sites, and resource sites. If it helps, print out their landing pages, home pages, and a secondary page from deeper in their site. Print out yours, as well, and lay all the prints side by side. How does your site design stack up? Does it look as professional as the other sites? Does it have a similar feel? Ask friends and colleagues for their opinions, too.

Include those excellent references

Include third-party sources who praise your company, service, or product. Industry awards, TV, newspaper and magazine quotes, certifications, and customer testimonials are all great. Ideally, you've selected them carefully for the best impact on the target audience. Avoid the temptation to overwhelm the page—and visitors—with references. Select up to three of the most compelling, and don't let them clutter the conversion path.

webex.com

This redesign of one of WebEx's highest volume landing pages yielded a conversion increase of 50%.

Note the PC Magazine Editor's Choice icon in the lower left: this is an excellent example of a third-party endorsement that helps establish credibility.

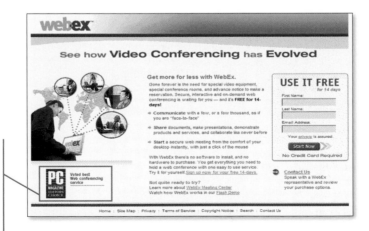

Ensure everything works

Obvious display problems or functional errors—broken image references, misaligned displays, typos, and broken links—suggest to visitors that your company has equally slipshod manufacturing or service habits.

Simplify and separate

Until recently, companies created landing pages conforming to the site's overall design, including the standard site header and navigation. It's more effective, however, to simplify the landing page and separate it from the main site—visually and architecturally.

Why is this approach effective? It encourages the visitor's attention to focus on your offer. Think of a landing page as a place to showcase your offer, like putting a spotlight on a Lamborghini or surrounding a diamond ring with a swirl of blue velvet. Instead of seeing distractions that have nothing to do with the immediate offer, visitors see what is most important.

Reduce or eliminate navigation

"Why would I create a page without navigation? I want people to see ALL the fantastic content and choices we offer."

No, you don't. People aren't coming to a site to see *everything* it offers, they're looking for the one thing they're seeking at that moment. This is especially true if you successfully drive targeted, well-qualified search traffic to a landing page. The most important, helpful thing you can do for visitors? Make it very clear you offer exactly what they want, then get out of their way so they can act.

Of course, it's possible to go too far in limiting choices:

Reduce branding and other standard site elements

"But why," you ask, "would I create a page without my big beautiful logo and site header graphics? I want to make sure people know who we are."

While it's true you want to retain some branding for identification and credibility reasons, at this point a company's identity is secondary to the offer. Devote as much real estate as possible to the offer. Also, there's no need to match a site's design literally. If you use a smaller logo and retain key branding elements like the company color palette, font treatments, and other branded motifs, visitors will effortlessly make the connection.

vonage.com home page

This home page includes standard, site-wide elements like full-size branding, complete navigation, login area, and search box.

vonage.com landing page

This example shows excellent landing page separation. Design and branding elements are consistent with the main site, but the layout and user experience is dramatically different.

Note how the landing page doesn't have the main site header or navigation bar. Vonage has consciously limited the available choices, making it easier to focus and act without distraction.

Make the landing page an extension of your ad

Many companies use templated landing pages. That is, they develop a single layout template, and then reuse it for an assortment of ad campaigns with slight differences in appearance, offer, and call to action. The reason for this is usually economic. After all, landing pages cost time and money to produce, and reusing a basic template saves resources in the short term.

But this approach ignores the importance of a consistent, seamless experience. To smooth the way for visitors, make the landing page an extension of the ad. This applies to the ad content, call to action, design, and tone.

Provide what the ad promised

Even the most forgiving visitor will be taken aback if you offer apples in your ad but carrots on your landing page. It's annoying to respond to an ad, only to discover the advertised item isn't in the store. At best, visitors will think they made a mistake by clicking the wrong ad. At worst, they'll think your company is incompetent or pulling the old "bait and switch" routine. Either way, you just lost a potential customer.

T-Mobile banner ad

The landing page for the above banner ad

tmobile.com

This banner ad's offer of "Unlimited calling from home just $9.99" is not repeated on the landing page. This is likely to make visitors hesitate as they look for the offer, then leave.

The moral of the story? If an ad offers a free white paper on processor speed comparisons, make sure that's exactly what's available on the landing page. The additional conversions are worth the extra effort.

Match the wording of the ad's call to action

Another fine point that makes a difference: match the wording of the ad's call to action as closely as possible. If an ad says "Free Trial Offer," repeat the phrase in the landing page's call to action: "Get your free trial offer today." A mismatch between the ad's call to action and the landing page's creates hesitation and doubt in the visitor's mind.

Use consistent graphics and illustration

Did your marketing department create a cool new graphic treatment for your ad campaign? Make sure to use it on your landing page! Consistent imagery glues the conversion process together, creating an unbroken experience.

Maintain language and tone

Is your ad erudite and intellectual? Then don't speak hip-hop on your landing page. Tone and language consistency is as important as imagery for creating a seamless flow.

omniture.com

Omniture does an excellent job of maintaining consistency between ad and landing page: The offering is present and worded the same way on both, the call to action is consistent, and the same imagery and colors are used on both.

Omniture banner ad

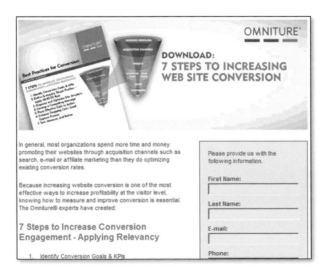

Omniture landing page

Offer segmenting options for different audiences

There is often no way to learn in advance the audience to which a visitor belongs. For example, if a visitor performs a search for a very general keyword such as "printers," it's impossible to tell from that search alone whether the visitor is a parent, a small business owner, or a purchaser for a large enterprise corporation. So how do you greet these unknown visitors? How do you address the specific questions and concerns of multiple audiences on a landing page?

One way is to offer *segmenting* options that allow visitors to prequalify themselves. A landing page with segmenting options includes a clear, audience-specific path for each of the most important audiences you anticipate will see the page, as in this example:

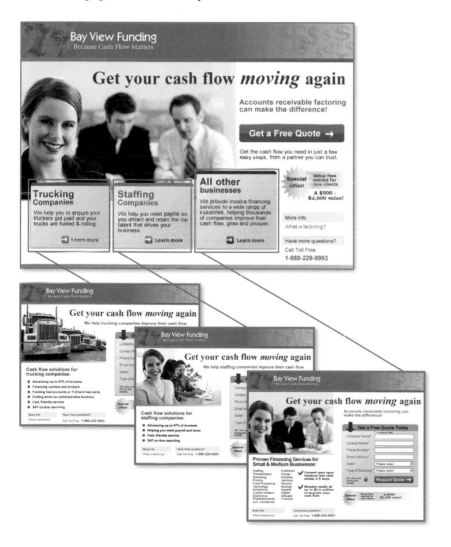

Segmenting:
Dividing customers into groups, each with common attributes.

bayviewfunding.com
This segmented landing page provides two audience-specific paths—one for trucking companies, another for staffing companies.

Clicking one of the segmented Learn More links leads visitors to an audience-specific page with targeted messaging and imagery.

To ensure other visitors also have a clear path, a more general All Other Businesses option is provided, which leads to a page with broader messaging.

Personalize to the visitor

Let's say you're trying to get the attention of a friend, Joe, who's standing some distance from you. Would Joe be more likely to respond to a general "Hey, you!" or to the more specific "Hey, Joe!"? Which would a crowd in Seattle prefer to hear from an entertainer: "Hello, there, everyone!" or "Hello, there, Seattle!"?

It's intuitive that when a communication is personally addressed to a specific audience it's more likely to create and build a connection with that audience. Snail-mail marketers have used this technique for years, inserting recipients' names into requests for donations and notices of sweepstakes winnings.

Landing pages can also benefit from this insight. Personalizing the look and wording of a landing page to a particular visitor or audience is a powerful way to capture and keep attention.

eloqua.com

This landing page for an email campaign is personalized with the visitor's first name.

carinsurance.com

This landing page is customized to speak to California drivers and their specific concerns.

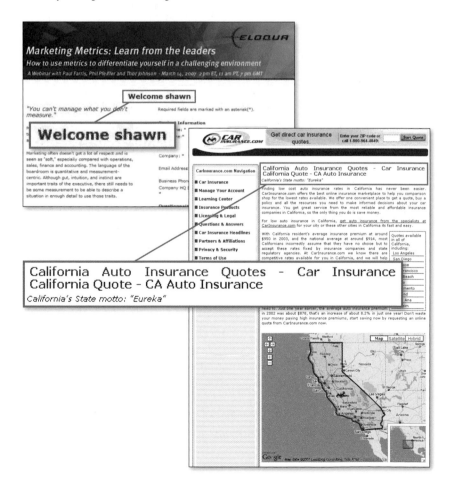

Use fewer, better graphics

Graphics have powerful uses on a landing page. They guide the visitor's eye in the desired direction, convey mood and company identity, and emphasize compelling aspects of your offer.

Too many graphics, however, confuse and distract. They divert attention from the message and slow visitor action. Buttons, icons, charts, diagrams, smiling-happy-people pictures, and especially flashy-twirly animated things: oh my! Every graphic element has the potential to overwhelm the call to action. Thus… reduce the number of graphic elements. Eliminate the nonessential. Don't decorate merely for decoration's sake.

netflix.com

Notable for what it doesn't include, this landing page has no images of DVDs, movie posters, TVs, or any of the things you might expect to see for a DVD rental company.

One strong image of a happy family watching a movie and a few other well-placed supportive graphic and text elements combine to create a high-impact landing page.

This page may look simple, but a lot of thought and effort clearly went into its design.

We're not advocating removal of all graphics, of course. The *right* graphics can clarify your offer and have a measurable, positive impact on landing page effectiveness. For instance: a diagram may instantly communicate what several paragraphs of text usually explain. A photo can answer questions, clarify new or difficult concepts, and display the product.

On the next page we compare the graphics used on four landing pages that are all attempting to communicate a fairly challenging concept—software that enables remote access to another computer:

gotomypc.com

In this image two widely separated computers connect and communicate with each other via electronic-looking signals. Fairly successful at communicating the concept.

pcnow.webex.com

Two computers are connected by a faint arrow and show the same screen display. Clearly one computer's content moves to another, but the concept of control is unclear.

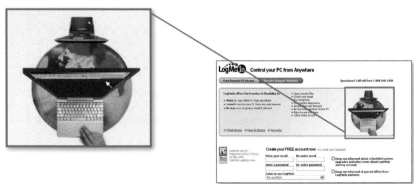

logmein.com

Two computers on a globe, one positioned as if the visitor is using it. The odd perspective makes it more difficult to grasp what this illustration is without some additional study.

symantec.com

An image of the software box, but no attempt to explain the concept. This is fine for visitors who already understand what the product does, but not for less experienced visitors.

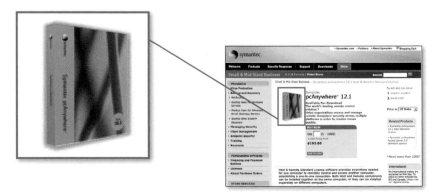

Choose the most effective media type for your offer

We discuss media choice in more detail in the Detail Pages chapter, but the key point to remember for landing pages is that the choice of a graphic also requires selecting the most effective media. By "media" we mean a range of visual presentation formats, including photos, illustrations, charts, videos, and animations.

Each media type has strengths and weaknesses. Photos are great for beauty shots but not very good for flowcharts. Videos and animations are terrific for demonstrations, but may be skipped or ignored by impatient visitors. It's important to consider which media type will communicate your offer quickly, clearly, and with the most impact.

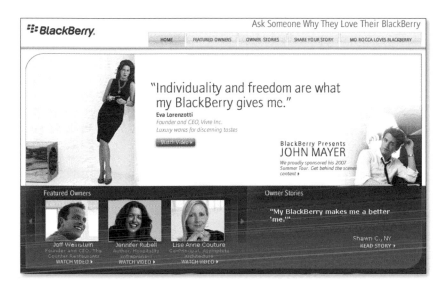

blackberry.com

This landing page combines static images and text with videos that begin playing when one of the buttons or thumbnail images is clicked. This provides immediate information to hurried visitors and a rich media experience for visitors who choose to linger.

Create interest and desire with compelling copy

Facts alone are usually not enough to make a sale. Important? Yes. Interesting? Yes. Compelling? Well…

Visitors arrive at your landing page already somewhat interested in its offer; after all, their arrival resulted from an ad click or e-mail link. Now they need a reason to continue, an emotional connection to overcome hesitation. Compelling copy connects customers to your offer.

How is this done? This is an area worthy of much in-depth discussion, but some key points follow.

Speak the customer's language

Don't use corporate lingo, technical jargon, or "marketing speak" and expect visitors to respond to it. What we've observed during user testing is that even minor phrase differences—for instance "auto insurance" instead of the more colloquial "car insurance"—can have a dramatic influence on whether visitors complete the desired action.

What does this mean for the landing page? Make sure its language matches the language of the target audience. If your target audience is internal sales-people, use cool brand names heavily; for an audience of CTOs use technical terminology. For general or multiple audiences, however, be sure to include the common terms for your product or service.

This concept also has applications specific to Paid Search advertising. When a visitor performs a search and clicks on your paid ad, they're sending a clear signal about how they think about your product. Ideally, the same search term they used—or something very similar—should show up in your paid ad and prominently on your landing page. This is a small but effective way to speak your visitor's language, immediately personalizing the offer and making it more compelling.

Engage the visitor with benefits, reasons, or scenarios they can relate to

This guideline encourages you to translate your offering into something more personal—something that could benefit your visitor's life. For example, if you're offering low-cost retirement accounts, show how much a typical person might save in fees over 10 years, and as a result, how much more money they'll have in their account by the time they retire. Answering the questions "What does my audience truly care about?" and "What problems does my offer solve for my audience?" will help you write truly compelling copy.

Include only the most important points

Your offer may have so many outstanding features it's physically painful to leave any off the list. Remember: you have limited space and time to make your point. Provide immediate answers to only the most relevant, motivating questions about your offer. Other questions can be answered elsewhere.

You have limited space and time to make your point. Provide immediate answers to only the most relevant, motivating questions about your offer.

Accommodate different reading patterns

Different visitors have different reading patterns, and your challenge is to provide enough compelling content for each pattern. Some visitors don't read at all; another reason to include at least one strong image. Some visitors read every word; for them provide enough solid detail to satisfy their inquiry.

Other visitors are somewhere in between. They scan headlines, maybe read the first couple of sentences. For these readers you need clear headlines that emphasize the benefits and important information early in each paragraph.

jennycraig.com

This landing page provides a variety of content that accommodates different reading patterns.

Key points are bolded within the detailed copy, allowing hurried visitors to quickly grasp the offer. Visitors who are less rushed or more detail-oriented have plenty of text to read.

Bold, scannable headlines communicate important information and pique interest.

Include the right amount of copy

How much copy is the right amount for your landing page? It depends on several things: the nature and complexity of your offer, your sales approach, and your audience's willingness to read on the web. If the offer is a commoditized product like a movie DVD, not much explanation is required, or desired. If the offer is more unusual, complex or specialized, then more description, testimonials, and examples are needed.

If the offer requires a significant amount of copy, a split presentation is an effective compromise:

- Above the *fold* place a condensed conversion area that includes your essential points, main call to action, and action area (a button, or a form plus button). This gives visitors who don't like to read a way to quickly scan the offer and take the next step.

- Below the fold, include more detailed information followed by another call to action and action area.

- Avoid a visual *false bottom* at the fold, or few people will scroll down. Arrange the page layout so at least one element—a graphic or a paragraph of text, for example—obviously crosses the fold-line.

- If copy is lengthy enough to require much scrolling, repeat the call to action and action area every 2–4 paragraphs, or once per visual "screen."

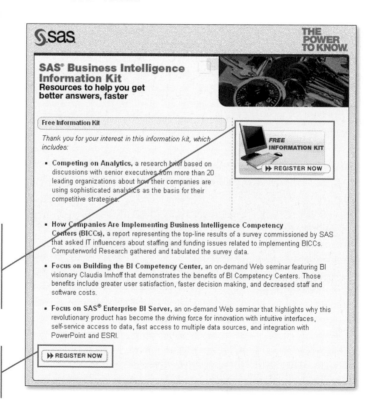

This approach addresses visitors at different stages of the sales cycle as well as those with different reading patterns. As with any guideline, we recommend testing and tracking results to see what works best for your product, company, and audience.

Fold:

The bottom edge of what a visitor can see of a web page without scrolling. A word originating in newspaper publishing.

False bottom:

An effect created when a web page appears to end at the fold, due to a significant visual gap in the design or content at that position.

sas.com

The SAS Business Intelligence landing page illustrates the use of repeated calls to action.

At the top of the page, an illustrated area repeats the benefit—Free Information Kit—and provides a button labeled Register Now.

At the bottom of the page, the Register Now button is repeated.

Provide a clear call to action

Visitors want you to show them where to go and what to do next. A clear call to action that's aligned with your ad's call to action makes it easy for them to see the path ahead.

Be clear, obvious, and concise

Your call to action is the essential focus of the landing page, the place where you make the visitor's next step perfectly clear. Trying to be subtle, clever, mysterious, long-winded, or timid at this point will hurt your landing page's effectiveness. Instead, make the call to action a concise distillation of all the elements in the ad and on the landing page. Headlines, copy, graphics, and charts should all support the actionable magic words, whether Register Now, Add to Cart, or something else.

Your call to action is the essential focus of the landing page, the place where you make the visitor's next step perfectly clear.

Avoid intimidating or unclear language

Some phrases sound more threatening, challenging, or difficult than others. Buy Now, for example, is often viewed warily, as if it may somehow be able to instantly debit money from one's bank account if clicked. Silly or not, this language often represents too high a threshold of trust and effort to expect from your visitor. Yet, we see calls to action all the time that make our hackles stand up, for instance: Send Us Your Personal Information.

A few more "bad calls" and why they're bad:

Bad Call to Action	Why It's Bad
"Make Your Dreams Come True!"	Too vague, difficult to accomplish
"Improve the quality of your life by buying our vitamins online today using our easy order form"	Much too long
"Start Celebrating!"	Too vague, and has nothing to do with the actual action needed to reach the celebration
"Buy Instantly!"	Too demanding
"Go!"	Unclear, and adds no reinforcement of the messaging

Provide a secondary, "safety valve" call to action

As you design your landing page, consider offering a *secondary call to action*. This is simply a fallback or "safety valve" alternate action the visitor can take if they don't wish to pursue the primary call to action just yet. The safety valve call to action is usually made less prominent on the landing page than the primary call to action, through the use of visual treatment, positioning, or both.

> "But I thought a landing page was all about focusing on a single goal! Why would I want to offer another, different action for the visitor to take?"

What if the visitor isn't ready to take your primary offer? Would you prefer to stick to your guns and lose a prospect entirely? Providing a secondary call to action allows you to have a partial win that continues some level of contact.

Some examples of complementary primary and secondary calls to action:

Primary Call to Action	Secondary Call to Action
"Add to Cart"	"Download a product brochure"
"Review Order"	"Questions? Chat live with one of our helpful team members"
"Download Trial Now"	"See Demo"
"Make Donation"	"Learn more about our mission"

Secondary calls to action are especially important if the primary call to action is complex, pricey, or requires a high level of commitment. The secondary call to action provides a simpler, easier path that makes the visitor more comfortable. For instance, if the product is expensive, offer a Download Product Brochure link.

And don't be afraid to provide offline alternatives. Many visitors are more comfortable talking to a live person on the phone than filling out an online form, so a phone number is an ideal secondary call to action.

Whatever your secondary call to action, be sure to implement tracking for these conversions along with your primary call to action conversions.

Before:

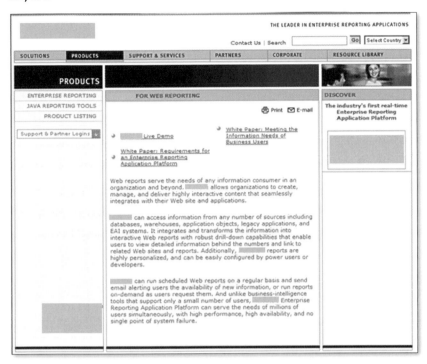

Old landing page

This landing page (branding is grayed out) included distracting navigation, dense blocks of text and unrelated options and promotions. The headline and desired actions did not stand out sufficiently to draw visitors' attention.

After:

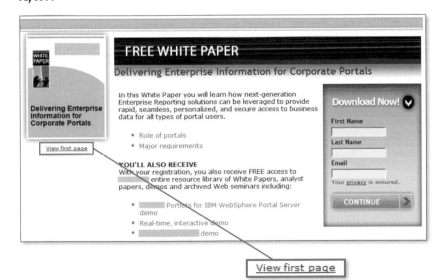

New landing page

This redesign incorporates a cleaned-up layout, simplified copy, a highly visible action area, and a clear call to action.

In addition to the other changes, a safety valve action, 'View first page,' allows visitors to preview the offer.

The result of this redesign? A 600% increase in conversions.

Keep form design clean and simple

We discuss form design in more detail in our Forms chapter, but some key points bear repeating here. Forms are intimidating enough without making them look unnecessarily complicated. Even complex forms can appear less difficult when they have a clean layout and simplified treatment. An "easy to do" appearance increases the odds the form will be completed.

Ask for the minimum amount of information you need

Reducing the number of fields in a form can dramatically increase its completion rate. So, take a hard, ruthless look at your form. Which fields are really necessary? How will each field be used? Is it truly vital, or just nice to have?

But wait. If your form lacks fields that are crucial lead qualifiers for your business you may trade too much lead quality for quantity. Deciding which form fields to keep is a balancing act. Too many form fields and the completion rate drops. Too few, and your sales team wastes time on poorly-qualified leads or you don't receive enough information to complete a transaction.

What we generally see, however, are forms with far, far too many fields.

Make buttons easy to find

A button is the tool visitors use to act, so why are so many buttons hard to find? We've heard live feedback from usability testing that will curl the hair of any web marketer:

- "Where's the Buy button? I can't find the Buy button!"
- "Well, I want to get to the next page, but how do I do it?"
- "I just can't figure out where to get started with this thing."
- "Oh, *that* button? No, I didn't see that one."

To avoid feedback like this, improve the visibility and clarity of your buttons with these guidelines:

Make buttons look like buttons

Like calls to action, buttons work best if they aren't subtle or mysterious. They should look exactly like what they are: buttons. This doesn't mean they have to be red rounded rectangles with a big drop shadow, but they

Take a hard, ruthless look at your form. Which fields are really necessary? How will each field be used? Is it truly vital, or just nice to have?

should be easy to distinguish from their surroundings, have enough buffer space to separate them from other elements, and look somewhat like a physical button.

Buttons That Look Like Buttons	Buttons That Don't
≫ **Add to Cart**	Add to Cart
Compare Prices	(COMPARE)

Make buttons large enough to read and click

Reading and clicking your buttons should not be a test of vision and dexterity. Of course, large button size can be taken too far, but we generally see buttons that are too small and hard to read.

It's easy to allow factors other than conversion—like available space in existing page templates, rigid design standardization, etc.—to drive button design. But the clickable action item on a landing page is one place where it's worth bending the standards. Give important buttons the size and legibility they deserve; they'll reward your attention with a better conversion rate.

Buttons That Are Large Enough	Buttons That Aren't
▶ View Flash Demo	GO
New Flight Search	Flights

Make important buttons more prominent

When we recommend making buttons large, we don't mean make every button look the same. Instead, important buttons should be more prominent than less important buttons. This can be achieved through size, color, placement on the page, or a combination of all three. Visitors should be able to tell at a glance which buttons corresponds to the most important actions on a page, which to less important actions, and so forth.

Use clear, concise, inviting labels

On landing pages, button labels often summarize the call to action. These labels should be clear, concise, and inviting. Take our quick button label quiz to see what we mean by this:

Button Label Quiz

For the call to action "Register for our free newsletter," which of the following button labels is the most enticing?

A) "Register"   B) "Register now"   C) "Get free newsletter"

If you answered C, you're correct! While all of the button label choices are clear and concise, C is the *most* specific and motivating.

Notice that the selection supports and reiterates the call to action, which is concise, clear, and enticing in its own right. "Register" and "Register now" are both clear, but they concentrate on the process (registering) rather than the much more interesting end result (getting a free newsletter).

Buttons with Clear Labels	Buttons without
Become a Member	Secure Register
Web Search	FETCH

Be clear about what's coming next

People like to know what to expect, and are annoyed if they don't find it. Your button labels and design set the appropriate expectation for your visitors, mentally preparing them for whatever comes next.

Setting expectations is especially important if a landing page is the first step to a multiple-step process. If you don't indicate the next step, you'll likely see a large dropoff rate.

Of course, it's possible to overdo it. For instance, there's usually no need to add explanations to common buttons for standardized procedures like Checkout and Search:

(overkill)

However, giving some indication of the process with a simple Continue is preferable to surprising the visitor.

Place buttons intuitively

A final note on buttons: Don't hide them! Even large, colorful buttons can be missed by visitors if they're in an unexpected location on the page. Place them in a visitor's natural scanning path. For most western visitors, this means the button that completes a process appears in the lower-right portion of your landing page.

For longer pages, place a button both above the fold and again at the end of your content, if your content extends below the fold.

Ideally, your overall landing page layout should guide the visual flow directly to the most important button, so visitors don't have to work hard to find it.

Putting it all together

We've talked about a lot of individual design elements. But how can you tell which combination of these elements creates the best-performing overall layout?

First, we recommend starting with a professional design. An experienced designer who really understands the importance of conversion will intuitively solve many design challenges. Next, test variations of the page against each other and compare results. One way to do this is by using a simple technique called *A/B testing*.

A/B testing:

A testing method by which a baseline control sample is compared to one or more varied samples.

Stop reading and try this...

FEATURED TECHNIQUE: A/B Testing

A/B testing can be used to compare the performance of two web page solutions. For instance, comparing the number of conversions Landing Page A generates compared with Landing Page B.

The concept is straightforward, but actually running an A/B test can seem daunting. Some companies have the technology and expertise to split incoming traffic between two pages; these organizations can set up and run A/B tests themselves. Those that don't can either hire a consulting firm to help, or run simple A/B tests themselves using a paid online ad platform such as Google AdWords or Yahoo! Search Marketing.

Here's how this would work: create two identical ads and link one to an "A" page, the other to a "B" page. This lets you use the ad platform's conversion tracking system to compare the two pages' performance. You'll need some expertise in one of these platforms, but they are relatively easy to learn and use—and less expensive than many other options.

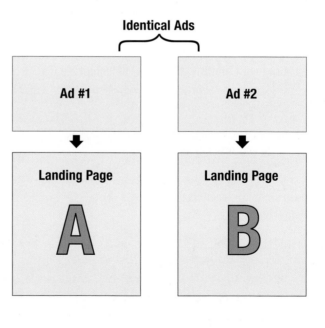

Considerations

To accurately compare page performance, the testing conditions must be equal for each page:

- **Identical ads.** Both ads must be entirely identical.

- **Visitor count.** Each page should receive an equal number of visitors. The total number of visitors included in the test should be statistically significant enough to provide reliable results.

- **Timing.** The ads should display during the same time of day, and the same days of the week.

- **Traffic source.** The ads should display in the same venues to ensure the resulting traffic quality is the same.

One test is not enough

Once you've run your first A/B test, don't stop there! An A/B test will tell you which of two options performs the best, but not whether you've reached the best possible solution. Take the test results and apply what you've learned to another test. And so forth, until testing and improvement are habitual elements of your site update cycle.

Learn more.

Google AdWords.
http://www.adwords.com

Yahoo! Search Marketing.
http://searchmarketing.yahoo.com

Summary

Landing pages play a crucial role in converting web visitors into customers. They welcome, communicate, and engage the visitor. They answer visitors questions, convince them of an offer's value, and provide a clear, easy path to the desired goal. When thoughtfully designed and coordinated with effective advertising, your landing page is one of your web site's superstars.

Let's look next at a page that often doubles as a landing page: your site's home page.

chapter 5

home pages

"There are three things you never want to see being made: sausage, law, and home pages..."

— *Sandra & Lance*

Historically, the home page was where most visitors began their experience with a web site. Over time this has changed.

Search engines have become more accurate, allowing visitors to find and go directly to deeper, more relevant site pages, for one thing. Online and offline advertising drives traffic to specific landing pages, for another. But the home page remains an important visitor gateway for most sites. Nothing too surprising about that.

What's surprising is that the home page is often the page where a high percentage of people leave (or exit from) a site. In our experience, most home pages have an *abandonment rate* of between 40%–60%* prior to optimization.

Let's think about what that means. Most organizations spend a lot of time, effort, and money building their web site and conducting marketing and public relations campaigns hoping to build a brand and drive traffic to their home pages. All this, only to have *half* of those who make it that far abandon the site without clicking a single link.

Abandonment rate:
The percentage of visitors who arrive on a page and leave (bounce) without navigating further into the site. Also known as a bounce rate.

* *Very large companies with well-known brands and large customer bases tend to have lower bounce rates on average.*

This phenomenon is so pervasive that we regularly start any conversion enhancement project by identifying the client's home page abandonment rate. And we usually find that it's quite high. So high, in fact, that when we present the figure to a web site owner for the first time, they tend to react with stunned glassy-eyed stares, as if considering seppuku*.

We find the figure appalling too, because home pages are often full of opportunities for small-effort, big-impact conversion enhancements. We've seen home page abandonment rates decline by 20 or more percentage points after full home page redesigns.

And when that 20 points of increased home page traffic cascades through the rest of a site, the net impact on metrics is substantial. How substantial? Let's look at two examples.

Example 1:

Home Page Visitors	OLD Abandonment Rate	Number of Visitors Who Explore Your Site
10,000	65%	3,500

Example 2:

Home Page Visitors	NEW Abandonment Rate	Number of Visitors Who Explore Your Site
10,000	**45%** (20% Reduction)	**5,500** (57% Increase)

*Here we can see how reducing the home page abandonment rate by 20 percentage points gives you a **57% increase** in traffic to the rest of your site. Of course, this represents an increase to the number of potential sales and other conversions on your site, as well.*

* A suicide ritual, historically practiced by Japanese Samurai, usually undertaken as a means of retaining honor in the face of disgrace.

Visitor Questions

Because a home page can be visitors' first interaction with the site, many of their questions pertain to credibility and relevance. Here are some typical home page questions:

- Is this what I expected to see?
- Does this look credible and trustworthy?
- What does this company do?
- Does this site offer what I want?
- Does this look interesting enough to spend more time here?
- What actions can I take now?
- Hmm... that's intriguing. How do I learn more?
- How do I contact the company?

Home Page Goals

The primary conversion goal for home pages is to persuade visitors to stay and click at least one link. Put another way, the goal for the home page is to convince visitors *not to leave*. Are we setting the bar too low? No, it's an acknowledgement of the "jumping-off-point" role the home page plays for most visitors.

Visitors, especially first-time visitors, don't arrive at a home page immediately ready to transact with a company, nor do they expect to do so. They expect to click around a little to find exactly what they want.

Online marketing guru Nick Usborne* likens the relationship between site owner and site visitor to a blind date, where people meet and get over some initial awkwardness before getting to know each other—and certainly before getting serious. To take this analogy further, web visitors want to know they're dealing with someone they like and trust before moving toward the intimate acts of purchasing or sharing personal information.

Yet we see many sites with overly loud Buy Now, Click Here, Join Today, and similar buttons on their home pages. These can be seen as the online equivalents of asking for a kiss before you finish introducing yourself.

See Nick's site at www.nickusborne.com.

Key Metrics for Home Pages

There are certainly a number of metrics you can use to monitor the success of your home page design, but we think these are the critical ones:

- **Home Page Abandonment Rate.** The percentage of people who land on your home page and leave the site without clicking further.

Example:

Say you have 10,000 unique visitors to your home page in July. Of those 10,000 visitors, 6,500 leave without clicking further into your site. Your home page abandonment rate is

$$6,500 / 10,000 = 65\%.$$

And for those "glass is half full" types, we offer...

- **Home Page Penetration Rate.** The percentage of people who land on your home page and *do* click at least one link. This is the opposite of the Home Page Abandonment Rate.

Example:

Say you have 10,000 unique visitors to your home page in July. Of those 10,000 visitors, 3,500 click at least one link on your home page further into your site. Your home page penetration rate is

$$3,500 / 10,000 = 35\%.$$

Considerations

It's ideal if you can break out your metrics by traffic source, as this allows you to isolate changes in your overall abandonment rate to one or more specific sources.

- **The effect of traffic quality.** Your home page abandonment rate will fluctuate in response to variations in your traffic mix. Just as with landing pages, driving a high volume of traffic from low-quality sources such as banner ads can reduce your conversion rate. Consider whether the volume of traffic offsets this reduction.

- **Specific versus aggregate metrics.** It's ideal if you can break out metrics by traffic source, as this allows you to isolate changes in abandonment rate to one or more specific sources. In addition, it's helpful to keep track of aggregate metrics and watch their trends over time to ensure you're heading in the right direction overall.

Unique Issues for Home Pages

The home page is often far removed from the actual conversion events, which normally take place elsewhere in the site. This position contributes to the challenges home pages face.

It must be everything to everyone

Like landing pages, home pages must perform many functions simultaneously. But home pages have a tougher job because they must meet the needs of a broader spectrum of audiences. While landing pages often target only potential customers, home pages must meet the needs of all the different audiences who may visit a site, including:

- Potential customers
- Current customers
- Press/Analysts
- Partners (current and potential)
- Investors (current and potential)
- Employees (current and potential)

Each audience will arrive at your home page with vastly different wants, needs, and expectations. And, like it or not, they will form judgments about your organization based on their experience with your site. To be effective, the home page must present the right image and give each audience a good reason to think they can find what they're seeking.

Predictably, many site owners and managers react to the challenge of designing a multifaceted home page by cramming it with as many options as possible, hoping visitors will find at least one option interesting enough to click. But visitors don't read every link on a page and are easily overwhelmed by too many choices. They'll quickly abandon a site that looks too complicated to decipher.

Visitors will quickly abandon a site that looks too complicated to decipher.

It is often highly political

It is a sad fact of life that home pages are the sacred cows of thousands of organizations. Admire them, appreciate them, but never tamper with them lest one wish to endure censure from one's colleagues and managers. Company after company willingly allows us to rip apart and rebuild their landing pages, product pages, shopping carts, and more, with good (often great) results. But when it's time to address the home page, we're often shut down, usually for "political reasons"—code for "The CEO likes it this way, so I'd be risking my job to suggest anything different."

A typical client response goes like this: "Yes, I see that our home page abandonment rate is 70%, and I appreciate the well-researched recommendations supported with hard metrics and case studies that you've provided us, but we can't change the home page now. The Home Page Committee only meets every other year, and they just met last month. I'll certainly bring this up at the meeting two years from now, though."

Which is when *we* start thinking about seppuku.

While we advocate a more rational approach to web site management and home page design, home pages are so invested with ego, emotion, and perceived significance that they can be difficult to change. If this is true for your organization, it makes sense to focus your conversion enhancement activities elsewhere first. Having other conversion "wins" helps shift attitudes and build your authority better than anything else. After all, it's hard to say no to someone who reports:

> "The changes we made to the product pages and shopping cart/checkout process yielded another $4 million in annual revenues. I think a focused home page redesign could yield another $2 million a year."

When your organization is ready to take on the challenge of redesigning your home page so that it's friendlier to visitors, the following design guidelines will help ensure success.

Home Page Design Guidelines

The following guidelines are presented in more or less the order in which visitors experience a home page.

First, visitors make a very quick, unconscious judgment about the site, based on the overall "look" of the home page.

Next, if the site passes this initial judgment, visitors look to verify they're in the right place and that the site offers what they need. This is affected by what options are present on the home page, and how they're displayed.

Finally, visitors look for clues about where things are on the site so they can get around more easily. This is affected by the site's navigation and display conventions. We also discuss the "tone" of your text, which can set a company apart and affect a visitor's experience.

It's hard to say no to someone who reports, "The changes we made to the product pages and shopping cart yielded another $4 million in annual revenues."

Before we dive in, however, don't forget to...

Start with landing page fundamentals

As we discussed, one of a home page's many functions is as a landing page for new visitors. This means many of the guidelines from our Landing Pages chapter will also apply to home pages, especially the following:

- **Establish credibility.** More on this follows, from a home page angle.

- **Meet expectations.** As we've discussed, the expectations for a home page are usually more diverse than those for a landing page.

- **Write compelling copy.** While your home page may not have much text, the copy you do have establishes the tone of the entire site.

- **Have clear calls to action.** On a home page, calls to action are more effective if they're softer and oriented more toward guidance than sales.

- **Use big, clear buttons.**

Establish credibility—look like what you are

Did you know visitors will decide whether your site and company are credible during the first second after they arrive? It's true. This decision will be made before they have time to scan your navigation labels or read your introductory text, before they learn how many services you offer, or click their first link.

How is this decision made? By the first *visual "hit"* visitors get from your home page. If your home page's appearance doesn't match their expectations for your industry and company identity, you're likely to bounce visitors like a trampoline.

While there's no single right "look" for each industry, heaven forbid you look like, for instance, a video game site if you're a mortgage lender! Would you still get customers? Probably a few who're impressed with your youthful hip-ness. But for most visitors, especially first-time visitors, that initial impression would be irreconcilable with their expectations.

To illustrate this point, we've pulled in home page examples from four widely different industries. Notice how each home page has a unique design, yet those within the same industry are more similar to each other in overall look and style than they are to sites from different industries (see next page).

Did you know visitors will decide whether your site and company are credible during the first second after they arrive? It's true.

Visual "hit":
The immediate impression or impact a site design has on a visitor.

Soft drinks

These home pages have in common an informal, youthful layout with plenty of animated, interactive elements, and lots of strong, eye-catching colors. Branding and image are emphasized.

coca-cola.com

mountaindew.com

pepsi.com

drpepper.com

Financial/Investment

These home pages have in common a traditional approach to page layout, a relatively restrained use of colors, and minimal or no use of animated elements. Information dominates the feel of these text-heavy pages.

schwab.com

fidelity.com

ml.com

tdameritrade.com

army.mil

airforce.com

navy.mil

uscg.mil

Military

These home pages have in common an overall serious, restrained look influenced by the use of relatively muted colors. Traditional columnar layouts predominate, as does the expected military imagery. These pages communicate a sense of sober pride.

ostcclauder.com

shop.elizabetharden.com

maybelline.com

revlon.com

Cosmetics

These home pages have in common a heavy use of striking imagery and light use of text, with layouts similar to print advertisements. Glamour, beauty, and brand are highlighted.

Clearly identify yourself and what you do

An important part of a home page's visual "hit" is your branded identity: the logo. Unless a company is an established brand (like the examples above) a logo alone may not be enough to identify it. Some basic identity questions to ask are:

Is your logo clear and legible?

Many logos suffer from legibility problems when transferred to a low-resolution existence on the web. Shrinking them to fit a reasonable amount of home page real estate only exacerbates the problem. Make sure yours can be read easily and quickly, even at a small size.

Shrunk to illegibility.

Over-designed and impossible to scan.

Is your logo visible?

"Visible" simply means easily seen. The best logo in the world won't help if visitors don't see it. For placement, the accepted web standard in western countries is the upper left of a home page. Okay, okay, we know: that may be boring. And yet, it's where the vast majority of western visitors will automatically look to find a logo—so why disappoint them? It's an easy way to keep them reassured.

Does your logo describe what you do?

Many company names and logos include a description of their business. For instance, "Ray's Plumbing" is self-descriptive and needs no further explanation. "RayCo," on the other hand, needs some annotation.

Do you need a tagline to describe what you do?

If there's a possibility your visitors could look at your logo and not instantly understand what you do, you need a *functional tagline*. We're not talking about a marketing slogan. Using a snappy slogan to convey a mood, attitude, or feeling is fine for advertising campaigns, but not when quick, laser-sharp communication is needed. On the web, a tagline performs a function similar to strip mall signage.

Make sure your logo can be read easily and quickly, even at a small size.

Functional tagline:

A concise, easily understood description of what an organization does.

The need for instant clarity is why strip mall signs typically leave off slogans and even brand names, opting for descriptive labels like "Chinese Food" and "Nail Salon" in big black letters, with brand names like "Chang's" and "The Hands Have It" in small cursive (if at all).

For example, which of these two signs is best at telling you there's an auto repair shop nearby?

"Huh? What does that mean?"

"Ah-ha! An auto repair shop!"

To further illustrate the difference between a marketing slogan and a functional tagline, here are some comparison examples:

Marketing Slogan	Functional Tagline
"Get a piece of the rock"	"Insurance and wealth management services"
"Just"	"High fashion clothing for women"
"It's what we do"	"Builders of opto-mechanical planetarium projectors"
"One step ahead"	"Products for babies 0–3 years old"
"No BS. No Hype. Just Results."	"Fitness equipment and training for men"

What if you *must* use your marketing slogan?

If there's a compelling reason for using a marketing slogan near your logo—for instance, if it's an integral part of your company's established identity and it's on all the canvas gym bags you passed out at Christmas—then include a functional tagline prominently *somewhere* else on the home page. It should be easy to find, easy to read, and super-clear.

Meet expectations—feature important items

Web surfers want to get straight to it, whatever "it" is. So make it easier for visitors to get to what they're looking for; put your most important items on the home page.

You may ask: "But, of all our great products, services, and information, how do we decide which are *most* important?"

There are a number of ways to prioritize your home page offerings, including these approaches:

Consider what *visitors* want to see

Ideally, always try to anticipate and meet your target audiences' needs and questions. Typical wins in this category include:

- Best-selling and most-requested products
- Items and services advertised on national TV, radio, or other non-web medium. Why? Because visitors may not have written down the marketing URL but did remember the company name, ending up at the home page.
- Links to information that answers anticipated questions
- How to contact you
- How to find support
- Where to login

Consider what *you* think is important

Having been entrepreneurs ourselves, we want to take a moment to acknowledge the importance of courageous vision, instincts, and going outside conventional wisdom.

We have, however, one addition to this approach: trust your gut, but verify. By all means, take chances, fly like an eagle and swim with the sharks. All we ask is that when you climb out of that shark cage, allow metrics to tell you which instincts are worth further investment and which just aren't panning out. Without some sort of testing and validation cycle, the home page is vulnerable to design driven by ego and politics, rather than accountable—if visionary—strategy and verifiable goals.

Allow metrics to tell you which instincts are worth further investment and which just aren't panning out.

Consider what *competitors* think is important

There's nothing wrong with using ideas from successful companies who've had to struggle with similar challenges. Beware of being derivative, however. There's no guarantee a strategy, design, or color scheme that succeeded for a competitor will translate well for your site or company. Not only could you lose the competitive differentiation so important to your identity, you could unknowingly repeat a huge mistake—which, believe it or not, even giants of industry have been known to make. Differences in strategy and audience can also reduce the effectiveness of a leveraged approach.

Consider what *customer feedback*, *surveys*, or *focus groups* tell you is important

This type of feedback can provide valuable insights. Remember, though, customers are notoriously inaccurate at predicting and remembering their real actions. Also, don't forget the feedback you're NOT getting. For instance, you won't be hearing from any visitors who left your site too irritated to swing by the customer service page or fill out a survey form.

Consider what *metrics* show you is important

A site's metrics are an important measure of what visitors are doing and looking for on the site. Certain site metrics in particular can help inform home page feature choices:

- **Hot sellers.** Online purchase or signup statistics show you which items are currently most appealing to your visitors. Feature these items on your home page and link to them.

- **Most visited pages.** Server log data reveals which pages are visited most frequently. Consider adding links to these pages on your home page.

- **Keyword searches.** External and on-site search term data tells you what visitors are looking for on your site. If any search terms stand out as being frequent and popular, provide clear, obvious links to items related to these terms.

Examples

Every company has to wrestle with choices about what to put on their home page, balancing business goals, branding, and visitor experience. On the next page are examples of what two successful but very different companies decided was important and appealing enough to put on their home pages:

> *There's no guarantee a strategy, design, or color scheme that succeeded for a competitor will translate well for your site or company.*

gametap.com

Gametap understands that conversion usually doesn't occur on the home page. Instead of trying to close the deal on the doorstep, a high number of enticing options gently lure the visitor deeper into the site.

Note the type of language that isn't here: hard-sell phrases like Buy Now, Sign Up, Register, Join. These tactics can backfire on a home page and increase the abandonment rate. The hardest sell on this page is Play Now, and we suspect few visitors will see this offer as intimidating.

The use of eye-catching motion and active language, such as Learn About, See it, and Browse transforms most elements into calls to action.

Proven means of generating visitor interest, such as surfacing Special Offers and Most Popular items, are displayed in a clear, appealing manner.

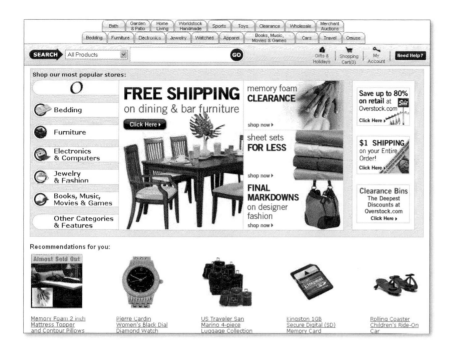

overstock.com

This home page provides a wide variety of enticing ways to enter and explore the site, including a top-level category list, special offers of various types, and recommended items.

The list of product categories provides quick, easy access to popular areas of the site.

Calls to action use mild, non-intimidating language—Click Here and Shop Now.

Special offers are front and center, some couched in language that indicates a sense of urgency without being too strong.

The next example illustrates the importance of not only placing important items on the home page but also making sure they are properly prioritized. The most important items should receive the most visual prominence, while items of lesser importance receive less emphasis.

Before:

Old home page

At first glance the old home page appears adequate. Most of the same elements are present here and on the new page, but here the information hierarchy is less clear and the main action area does not immediately attract visitors' attention.

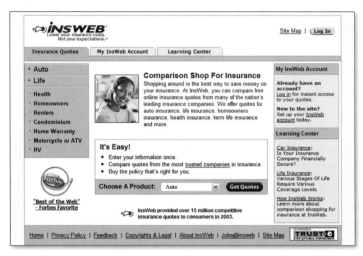

After:

New home page

The redesigned home page created a more professional feel, and resulted in a 25% increase in click-throughs to the insurance quote application.

The left-hand product link labels were updated to be clearer.

The benefit statement and entry point to the insurance quote application are more prominent and scannable.

Make your navigation easy and intuitive

When visitors arrive at your home page, they need to quickly "get" how the site is organized and how to navigate. Why? Because if visitors understand where things are, they feel more in control, more comfortable, and are more likely to explore successfully, finding what they want.

Use a standard navigation scheme

For your "persistent" or main site navigation, stick to one of the standard navigation placements:

- Across the top
- Down the left side
- Top and left combined. In this instance, often the more general options such as Product Categories, Contact Us, and Customer Service are placed across the top, and the more specific options like subcategories or individual items are listed down the left.

An alternative navigation scheme, such as listing main navigation choices down the right rail or scattering them artfully across your home page, works mainly for niche audiences expecting a more stylized approach.

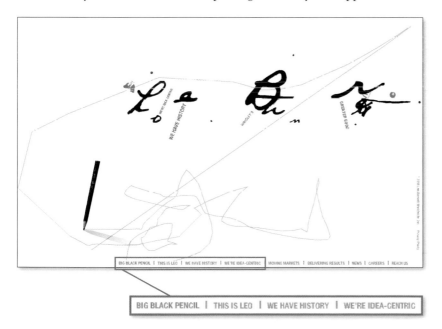

leoburnett.com

Even niche audiences appreciate clear, easy-to-use navigation. The advertising giant Leo Burnett's site is phenomenally creative, but navigating the site with the pencil-like cursor while all the page elements move around is difficult and counter-intuitive. We're certain the later addition of some static text elements to the page footer increased the site's penetration rate.

Stop reading and try this...

FEATURED TECHNIQUE: Card Sorting

Card sorting:

A technique used to investigate how typical visitors would group and label the items on a site.

It is a deceptively difficult challenge to group items together so they make sense to visitors, and label these groups or categories clearly and reasonably so everyone understands them. If a site is complex, or it's not clear how certain items should be grouped, a technique known as *card sorting* provides insight into how typical visitors would group and label the site items.

Prepare by getting a set of 3" x 5" cards. On each card, write one item that is (or will be) included on your site. These could be products you sell on your site, services you offer, or the titles of different information pages. You can limit the scope of this exercise to a single section of your site, or include your entire site. Either way, make your card set as complete as you can.

Once you have your card set ready, gather a group of people who are representative of your site's audience and give each person a copy of your card set. Ask each to sort the items into related piles and then label the groups. Have each helper work individually, without consulting the others.

Emphasize to your helpers that you are not testing them in any way, and there is no "right" way to group the items. Rather, they are helping you understand how visitors might expect your site to be organized.

A card-sorting session might start with an ungrouped list of items such as:

... and result in labeled groups like this:

Living Room
Sofa
Lamp
TV

Kitchen
Sink
Oven
Toaster

Bedroom
Bed
Dresser
Pillow

Learn more:

Usability Net.
http://www.usabilitynet.org/tools/cardsorting.htm

Include search capability and a site map

Many visitors prefer to search instead of clicking. Nearly everyone who uses the Internet is familiar with searching; not only are search engines widely used to search the web, nearly all of the most heavily-visited websites provide on-site search as a standard feature. So why should visitors have to spend time learning a site's particular navigation scheme if they prefer to search? They shouldn't. Provide a search box on the home page, and make sure it works well.

Other visitors prefer a site map that offers a quick "you are here" overview of every major section of the site on a single page. While many sites provide a site map as part of their *search engine optimization (SEO)* efforts, we've seen how important it can be as fallback navigation, and recommend making the site map visitor-friendly and linking it from the home page.

Search engine optimization (SEO):

Making web sites and their content friendly to search engines, in order to achieve higher rankings in search result listings.

verisign.com

This site map provides easy access to all the major areas of the site.

Establish conventions

Establish a convention:

Create a set of generally accepted standards through recurrent use.

Your home page is where you *establish conventions* for your site. Ideally, your home page will provide a visual "key" to identify different types of information at a glance, so visitors can easily find what they need, and tune out the rest. Conventions can take many forms, including location, color, size, font, or a combination of all of these.

The YouThink site offers a good example of establishing a convention using color as a visual indicator. Each topical area on a page appears within its own color, and deeper pages continue this convention.

youthink.worldbank.org

Green is used to indicate "Featured Issues."

Reddish-orange is used to indicate "Get Involved" items.

Purple is used to indicate "Multimedia" resources.

This home page establishes the convention of placing contextual, relevant links at the upper right of the page. Deeper pages continue this convention.

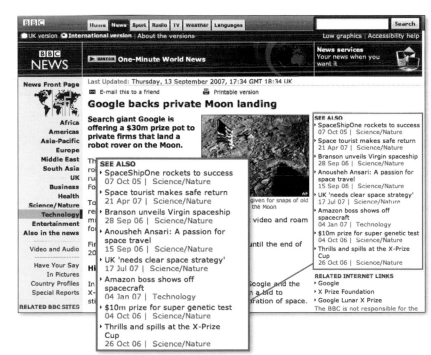

On this article page, contextual links appear in the upper right column, just as they did on the home page. Because this treatment is familiar from the home page and is used consistently throughout the site, visitors quickly learn to look here for other similar items of interest.

Establish your organization's tone

Many home pages don't have a lot of text. They're too busy doing all the other things we've been discussing. But for those that do include text, establishing a distinctive, consistent copywriting tone is key to supporting a company's identity and credibility.

traderjoes.com

This site quickly distinguishes itself from traditional grocery stores through design and home page copy. The breezy, friendly tone communicates a sense of personality that continues throughout the site.

WELCOME TO TRADER JOE'S, your neighborhood grocery store. A quick trip through our island paradise - um, website - will tell you a little bit about who we are, how we do business and, most importantly, where to find the Trader Joe's in your neighborhood. 'Cause that's where the value, adventure and tasty treasures are discovered, every day. Thanks for stopping by.

Summary

As we've noted, conversion events may rarely occur on home pages, but home pages play a critical role in determining a site's overall success. A well designed home page amplifies a site's effectiveness, whereas a poorly designed home page chokes off a site's conversion funnel at the top by limiting the number of visitors who make it further into the site where conversion really happens.

Let's look deeper into the site now, and consider a page type that visitors are likely to see next when navigating from a home page—category pages.

chapter 6

chapter 6

category pages

"We would have been happy if we could have assigned just three categories, large, medium, and small... It actually turned out to be quite a finely tuned scale."

— *Charles Francis Richter, creator of the Richter earthquake magnitude scale*

Category pages are an under-appreciated part of the conversion process because when well planned and designed, they are almost invisible to visitors.

They do a lot of cool sophisticated things, but they do them so neatly and intuitively that visitors race through them like a relay runner grabbing the baton. And that's exactly as it should be, because the conversion finish line usually lies ahead, not on the category page.

Category pages are essentially high-level filters, grouping items so that they make sense to the audience. With a click, large swaths of unwanted products or services can be pruned away, freeing visitors to lean in, look more closely, and consider the finer details. It's all about refining a wide range of choices down to just one—the one the visitor orders from you.

What's on an effective category page? Items or groups of items that are reasonably related to each other, for one. Basic information about each item, for another. And, finally, tools to slice, dice, sort, filter, and otherwise organize the items in ways that clarify the differences among them. Because if visitors can't see the differences, there might as well not be any.

With a click, large swaths of unwanted products or services can be pruned away, freeing visitors to lean in, look more closely, and consider the finer details.

Category pages are meant to practically fall over themselves to help visitors. A vision that comes to mind when we think of an ideal category page is a genial chef welcoming a favored visitor into her kitchen. "You want salad?" she asks. "I've got that for you, right here. You want to see all my salads with green and red ingredients? Voila! Want to see salad recipes sorted by country of origin? Sure thing. Would you prefer to see that list grouped by diet requirement? But of course: here are the first 20 of 55, just tell me when you'd like to see more, OK?"

And while our fictional visitor peruses the salad offerings, let's take a look at category page goals.

Typical Category Page Goals

The goal of a category page is to move visitors forward in the selection process. Depending on the type of offering and where a visitor is in the sales cycle, the next step in that process could be one of many options. Here are a few situations and what the likely next step is:

Situation	Likely Next Step
Visitor wishes to narrow the list of possible selections	Use of a tool to filter the selections by relevant criteria
Visitor wishes to see a quick subset of the possible selections	A click-through to a subcategory page
Visitor wishes to see which item has the lowest price	Use of a sorting tool to re-order the list of items
Visitor wishes to see a larger image and more in-depth information about an item	A click-through to a detail page
Visitor wishes to buy an item immediately	A click on an Add to Cart button

To motivate this step forward, category pages must successfully

- Present items in an attractive, appealing manner.
- Provide enough information for visitors to distinguish among items.
- Provide the means to sort and filter items by criteria that's important to visitors. The more complex or numerous the items, the more important this is.
- Provide a clear path to the next step.

Visitor Questions

Visitors arrive on a category page and quickly survey it for any sign of the item they seek. And, of course, they have questions that need answering.

- Is this what I expected? Did I pick the right category?
- How are these items sorted? By price? By color? Or something else?
- Can I rearrange them? How?
- Are there more items in this category? Where?
- I saw something a minute ago that I liked. How do I get back to it?
- There are a lot of items here. How do I narrow the list?
- Oops, I narrowed the list too much. Can I undo that?
- I see something I want. How can I buy it right now?

Key Metrics for Category Pages

In line with the main goal of a category page, the two most important metrics to measure on a category page are

- **Click-through percentage**. The percentage of visitors who click through to a subcategory or detail page.

Example:

In July, Category Page A receives 1,000 unique visitors. Of these visitors, 760 continue to a subcategory or detail page. The category page click-through percentage is

$$760 / 1,000 = 76\%.$$

And, if the category page provides an Add to Cart button for each item

- **Add to cart percentage**. The percentage of visitors who add an item to their shopping cart from the category page.

Example:

In July, Category Page B receives 1,000 unique visitors. Of these visitors, 230 add at least one item to their shopping cart from the category page. The category page add to cart percentage is

$$230 / 1,000 = 23\%.$$

Pogosticking:

The action of navigating back and forth between different site levels or search result listings.

Visitors often blame themselves for failing to find something on a site.

Considerations

- **Watch for *pogosticking*.** Visitors who click back and forth ("pogo-stick") between category and detail or subcategory pages probably aren't finding enough information to make a decision. This type of behavior can make it appear as though a category page has a high conversion rate when in reality it is performing poorly. If your analytics package provides views of visitor "paths" through a site, check for this pattern.

Unique Issues for Category Pages

Category pages can be unobtrusive helpers or literal roadblocks that prevent a sale or registration. Here are some of their issues.

They don't understand the audience

Visitors often blame themselves for failing to find something on a site. In fact, it's usually not visitors but the site's underlying information architecture that should be blamed. Sites that lack a good understanding of what visitors want to do and how they want to do it will generate categories that may seem logical but fail to meet visitors' needs.

This failure to understand can show up as an unexpected way of grouping things. Take, as an extreme example, a grocery store that groups everything by color. To find spinach, Comet cleanser, and St. Patrick's Day greeting cards, just visit the Green aisle! Logical? Yes, in a loony sort of way, but it's far too different from the way visitors expect a grocery store to be organized. Sure, they could shop there, but what a lot of extra effort it would take!

Sites also display a lack of audience understanding with poor category labeling. The failures we often see here are cutesy, marketing lingo labels that sound nice but obscure the contents of the category.

They're too rigid

Category pages can also miss the mark by not providing adequate filtering and sorting. In this scenario, the groupings are great and visitors easily find the right category—digital cameras, for instance. But once there, the only sorting option is price—high to low, and low to high. What about visitors who care about other criteria, like mega pixels, zoom, brand, or weight? Those visitors are gone, headed to a competitor with great sorting options that help close the deal.

What's happening here is more than simple inconvenience; inadequate comparison options actually force visitors to work harder. If a site doesn't identify important comparison criteria—like megapixels—visitors must think of them on their own. And if the site simply has inadequate filtering options overall, visitors must try to remember which items matched their criteria. Faced with a sense of much effort ahead, visitors in this situation often prefer to not choose anything at all.

Inadequate comparison options actually force visitors to work harder.

They're overpopulated

Site owners with a governing philosophy of "more is more" try to fit as many items as possible on a category page. "We have 500 storage containers!" they boast, "each of them a gem, not one to be missed!" This eager overabundance quickly degrades the clarity of a category page, confusing and annoying visitors instead of helping them compare and sift through their choices.

Category Page Design Guidelines

A helpful, clear category page is a true friend to the seeking visitor, making it easy to sift through a myriad of choices. Here are some guidelines to consider testing on your site:

Create categories that support how visitors think and act

We all agree categories should make sense, but category pages can do more than be merely logical. They can help visitors do what they came to do, in the way they prefer to do it.

How do we know how visitors prefer to do things? One technique to help uncover visitor wants and needs is to create *scenarios*. We describe this in more detail in the Featured Technique section later in this chapter.

Another approach is to leverage successful offline (brick-and-mortar) shopping models that are already familiar to your audience. The following two examples reflect well-understood offline shopping expectations for specific audiences (see next page).

Scenario:

A short story about a specific visitor with a specific goal while visiting a site. A scenario includes a brief description of the visitor and their recent circumstances, a statement of what task they wish to accomplish, why they want to do it, and what they expect. Scenarios often refer to a persona.

safeway.com

This store offers a Shop by Aisle category which displays groceries using groupings and labels that emulate a trip to a physical Safeway store.

armaniexchange.com

This site includes an effective and intuitive category called Looks, a kind of super-category of complete outfits. Clicking on a Look takes visitors to that outfit's category page where they can view the individual outfit pieces. This category supports the way many visitors prefer to shop for clothes—by outfit.

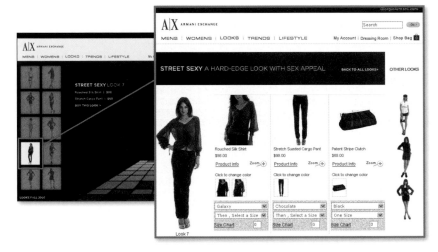

Make the category title obvious

After clicking a category link, visitors want assurance that they've arrived at the expected location; a large, obvious title above the category items helps.

cooks.com

This site includes large, easily read category titles at the top of the main content area.

Clearly define the category display area

What should be the focal point of a category page? The site navigation? A column of special promotions? Of course not, although the appearance of some sites makes that a reasonable assumption. Make sure category page items have their own distinct space, visually separated from other page elements. A quick glance should be all that's necessary to locate and begin scanning a category page's contents.

microsoft.com

There's a lot happening on this category page for Microsoft Word 2007 training courses, but the display area is visually separate from the branding, navigation, and advertising elements.

Clearly separate individual items

Separation is equally important for each item on the page. Provide adequate space and distinction between and around individual items so they're easy to distinguish and easy to click.

smithsonianstore.com

Each item on this page has a distinct, clearly defined space. This focuses visitor attention on the beautiful category contents.

Use clear, sharp, professional images

A category page thumbnail image may be the first look visitors have of your product, so make sure it represents it well. Because thumbnail images are small extra care should be taken to ensure they are clear and meaningful.

tiffany.com

Few sites take as much care with their product images as this site. The gorgeous, clean photography increases the allure and perceived value of the products.

Make thumbnail images large enough to identify the item

Many thumbnail images are woefully small and fuzzy, carelessly resized, or poorly cropped from a large image to fit the available space. This adds nothing to the appeal of an item, so make the image large enough to see what it represents. Better to present 20 easy-to-see items than 40 that are hazy and unclear.

istockphoto.com

Not only are the thumbnail images on this category clear and sharp to begin with, mousing over them generates a larger version in a popup layer. This is a convenient, easy way for visitors to preview and distinguish among the items, and a good solution to the limitations of a small image size.

Crop thumbnail images for relevance and meaning

When display size is limited, image content must be carefully selected for greatest relevance and impact. It is not always desirable to include the entire original photograph—or even the entire item—in a thumbnail image. This is where *relevant cropping* comes in. Select the most identifiable or distinguishing portion of your image and crop the rest away. This allows more of the relevant detail to fit within the thumbnail size restrictions. Here are some examples of what we mean:

Relevant cropping:
An image processing task that removes unwanted parts of an image to accentuate the subject or other important portion of the image.

Full Image (Large)	Full Image (Reduced)	Cropped for Relevance

Link thumbnail images

Visitors expect thumbnail images to be linked, and will click on them in hopes of continuing through to the subcategory or detail page. In addition, linked images are easier to click than text, and don't require reading to understand.

Provide options for display, sorting, and filtering

One of the most important services a category page provides is allowing visitors to compare and contrast items in a variety of ways. Items that are complex, such as electronic devices, or those that can be described or grouped in a wide variety of ways, such as food or decorative knick knacks, need more sorting and filtering options than simpler items.

Once again, an awareness of what questions the site's visitors ask about the item and how they prefer to group it will help determine what types of tools to offer.

gettyimages.com

This visual assets site is driven by filtered search rather than pre-defined categories. The results page acts as a dynamic category page.

General filtering options like image type and image orientation appear across the top of the page.

Contextual filtering options like Style, Location, and Keyword are listed down the left-hand side.

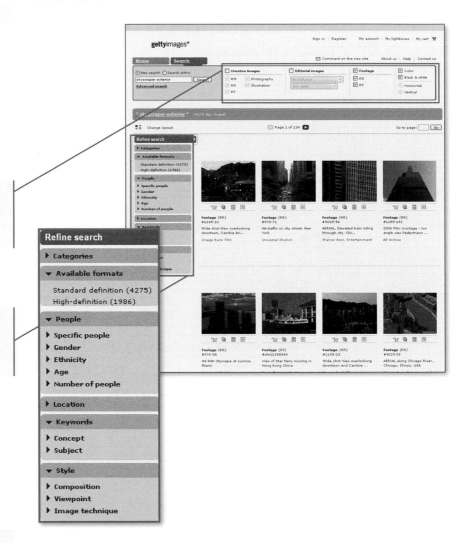

WEB DESIGN FOR ROI

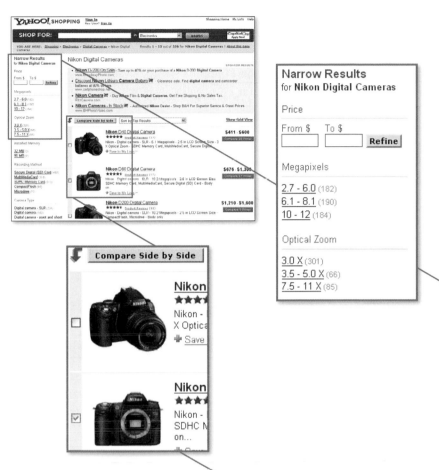

shopping.yahoo.com

This site provides a wide variety of tools to sort, filter, and display items. The tools are contextual, meaning they are relevant to the type of item being displayed.

In this example category— Nikon digital cameras—the filtering options include criteria such as Price, Megapixels, Optical Zoom, and Installed Memory that are specific to this category of items.

Alternate product views include a comparison view, allowing for side-by-side feature comparisons.

Exclude extraneous information

It's tempting to immediately reveal as many amazing details about your items as possible. But category page visitors aren't quite ready for a truck-load of detail. They're still in overview mode, narrowing their options a chunk at a time. Not only that, but too much detail gets in the way of scanning and comparing. It slows visitors down, making them try to take in too much information at once.

Rather than risk that slowdown, keep the category page details limited to what helps identify and clarify differences between items.

Clean and scannable:

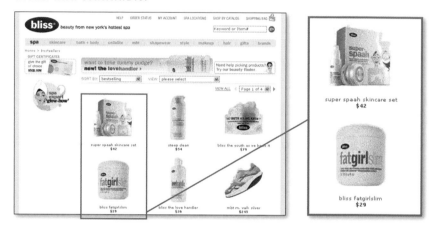

blissworld.com

This category page provides just enough information for each product to identify and distinguish it—image, brief descriptive title, and price.

Cluttered and distracting:

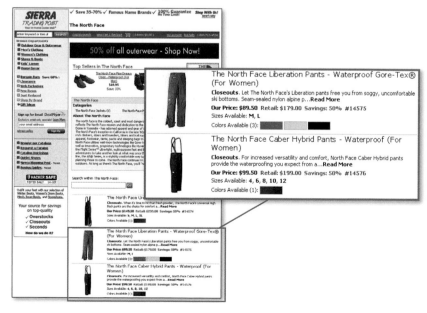

sierratradingpost.com

This category page clutters the page with a long text area describing the brand, pushing individual items below the fold on most monitors. Item listings provide so much information the page looks dense and difficult to scan.

Include a comparative price

Comparative pricing doesn't work for every site, but it can have a powerful influence for certain types of items. A comparative price highlights a sale, reinforces a member's sense of privilege, or provides easy comparison to competitor pricing. In other words, it makes an item look even more like a special deal.

For sites selling commoditized or highly competitive items, price is a critical factor that can make or break a conversion. Why encourage visitors to leave your site for a quick round of comparison shopping? Providing a price comparison on a category page helps retain and convert potential customers.

sportsmemorabilia.com

This category page includes a comparison between List Price and Our Price, making it clear what a deal visitors get by purchasing here. Another potential addition here would be a You Save amount, to further clarify the savings amount.

Consider including an Add to Cart button

Many sites follow a strict protocol regarding when a visitor may add an item to their cart (or bag, lightbox, or other prevailing site metaphor). "Only on the detail page!" is their rallying cry. And for many types of items it's the right thing to do. If items are difficult to tell apart, expensive or rare (therefore requiring a stronger sales pitch or additional information), or simply have options that must be selected prior to purchase, the category page is too soon to offer a purchase call to action. Also, if space is limited adding an action button may clutter the page and draw attention away from the category contents.

But for items that are easy to distinguish and simple to explain, why not save visitors a click?

proflowers.com

This category page is a good candidate for having a Buy Now button at the category level—the items don't require much explanation and are easy to distinguish from each other.

markys.com

The items on this gourmet food site are relatively easy to tell apart. Including a Buy Now button at the category level makes sense here, as well.

Putting it all together

In this chapter we've discussed a number of ways to improve the conversion performance of a category page. Foundational to all of these guidelines, however, is a thorough understanding of your audience, and on the next page we take a closer look at one technique to help you improve that understanding—developing scenarios.

Stop reading and try this …

FEATURED TECHNIQUE: Scenarios

Scenarios bring your visitors' goals to life with concrete examples. They help you focus on visitors, their questions, and the tasks they wish to accomplish while on your site, thus driving your decisions about site features, functions, and site architecture.

Scenarios can be simple or detailed, but are always stated from the visitor's point of view, rather than from a site functionality viewpoint. Ideally scenarios are supported and informed by actual audience data from such sources as interviews, usability testing, and site metrics.

Simple scenario examples:

- A business traveler wants to plan a trip from Phoenix to Atlanta next month. She needs a flight, hotel, and rental car.

- A college student wants to order pizza for delivery to his dorm room.

- A parent who is worried about the bee sting his five-year-old just received wants quick symptom and treatment information.

Detailed scenario example:

Persona: Business traveler
Task: Plan a trip

Susan is planning a trip from Phoenix to Atlanta next month. She needs a flight, hotel, and rental car. She has three days off for the trip. She has to be in Atlanta on the 17th for an afternoon business meeting, but is open on travel dates because she wants to visit her brother for a day or two during the trip. Her company is paying for the trip, so she's not too concerned with cost; she's most interested in getting a direct flight and a clean, quiet hotel that has a fitness center and is near her meeting location. She prefers Continental Airlines because she's a member of their frequent flyer program.

She needs a large rental car to accommodate her brother's three children on a trip for everyone to the local amusement park. She'd like to make all the arrangements today, but she has only 45 minutes during lunch to do it. She'll use a company credit card to pay for the reservations.

When to use scenarios:

Scenarios are helpful at various stages of site design and development. Typically, use simpler or more general scenarios at early stages of design and development, and very detailed scenarios at later stages or to guide solutions for complex tasks.

How many scenarios do you need?

The number of scenarios you create depends on the diversity of your site's audience and the complexity and depth of your site. Start with 10–30 scenarios, then step back and review them to see whether all important tasks and visitor types have been addressed. Too few scenarios and you will have an incomplete understanding of your audience's needs; too many and you'll be overwhelmed with too much detail.

Learn more:

Usability Net.
http://www.usabilitynet.org/tools/scenarios.htm

Usability.gov.
http://www.usability.gov/analyze/scenarios.htm

Summary

Category pages fulfill a pivotal—dare we say decisive?—role in helping visitors narrow their range of choices and move forward in the selection process. When well designed and in tune with audience needs, a category page provides a valuable service to visitors and a key contribution to a site's overall success.

Next up: the page many visitors will see after a category page— the detail page.

chapter 7

detail pages

"Anyone who says money can't buy happiness doesn't know where to shop."

— Mrs. Howell, Gilligan's Island

At last! Visitors have found what they were looking for and have arrived on the item's detail page, ready to buy. Success! Right?

Don't break out the champagne just yet.

Yes, some visitors will arrive here ready to buy with no further help. Many are still deciding. They might be comparing competitors' offerings in other browser tabs or windows, or pogosticking back to a category page or search engine results page to see if anything else looks interesting. They might be IM-ing friends, or reading a product review printed out earlier.

The point is you can't relax your conversion efforts. It's tireless work, and visitors may not be paying as much attention as you'd like.

How do you catch and keep visitor interest? How do you communicate your offering's value quickly, clearly, and attractively? How do you make it easy for them to accept your offer?

If those questions sound eerily familiar, almost as if we're talking about landing pages, they should. Detail pages, like landing pages, are often the first experience a visitor has of a site—especially if the detail pages are search engine optimized so they appear in online search results.

Let's look at some typical goals businesses have for detail pages.

Typical Detail Page Goals

The primary goal of a detail page is to persuade your visitor to accept your offer or to take the next step toward accepting it. Supporting this goal are sub-tasks that the detail page must perform effectively to achieve its primary goal, such as:

- Help visitors examine the offering more closely

- Answer any questions visitors may have

- Communicate any special features that distinguish the offer from competitors'

- Offer alternate purchasing methods, such as by phone

While these represent common examples, the selection of other sub-tasks needed on your detail page depends heavily on the expected audience and the offering itself.

Visitor Questions

Detail page visitors will be in different stages of the sales cycle, and their questions will vary accordingly.

Many arrive on a detail page ready to buy, looking for the Add to Cart button. Others are still in the "interest" phase of the sales cycle, researching the product. Review sites have made it easy to learn about product features and benefits online. So easy, in fact, that one major electronics retailer made headlines in 2007 by replacing 3,400 of its more experienced salespeople at its brick-and-mortar stores with less experienced (and lower-paid) service clerks. Why? To save money, of course. But the decision was also driven by customers arriving at the store with multiple web printouts in hand, needing less product information.

If people are relying so heavily on third parties for their research, does a detail page still need details?

Yes, because details add credibility and fulfill the needs of any visitors who haven't researched elsewhere. These visitors will want to read technical specs and see if the shipping costs are competitive.

The more complex the offering, the more detailed the provided information should be... while still keeping the path to purchase clear and easy to find.

If people are relying so heavily on third parties for their research, does a detail page still need details? Yes.

Let's take a look at potential questions visitors to the detail page have. Again, if visitors find the answers to any of these questions unsatisfactory, they are much less likely to convert.

Arrival questions

- Is this the item I expected to see?
- What does it look like?

Product questions

- What are the main features and benefits?
- How do I examine it more closely?
- What does it do, how does it work?
- What are its options, and how do they look?
- How do I select or change options?
- Is it available for purchase?
- What do other people say about it?

Price questions

- How much does it cost?
- Is it on sale?
- If there's no price shown, how do I get an estimate?

Extras

- Does it come with any accessories?
- What other items complement it?
- What shipping/return/warranty/support options are available?

Next step questions

- How do I buy or start the pricing process?
- What if I don't want to purchase it right now?
- What if I have more questions?

Key Metrics for Detail Pages

Similar to landing pages, detail pages have one metric that's most meaningful. This metric will be phrased differently depending on the page goal:

Page Goal	Key Metric	Example
Sell a product	"Add to Cart" percentage. The percentage of visitors that successfully add the offered item to their shopping cart.	170 unique clicks on the Add to Cart button on one detail page / 1,000 unique visits to that detail page = 17% conversion rate for that detail page.
Lead generation	"Lead Generation" percentage. The percentage of visitors that successfully complete the action required to continue to the next step in the process.	200 unique clicks on the Get Free White Paper button / 1,000 unique visits to that detail page = 20% conversion rate for that detail page.

Considerations

- **Alternate conversion paths.** If you provide an alternate sales or lead generation path on your detail page, such as a phone number or live chat tool, you'll want to track these conversions and attribute their origin to a specific detail page if possible.

- **A plethora of available metrics.** Of course, there are other metrics you could track on this page. You could look at how many of your cross-sell items are clicked. Or whether visitors download your services brochure PDF. Or how many e-mailed the page to a friend. We love metrics as much as the next marketing geek, but when it comes right down to it, the primary conversion is the metric that counts.

Unique Issues for Detail Pages

As we've already mentioned, detail pages must walk a fine line between providing too much and too little information. Other important issues for detail pages include:

They may also serve as landing pages

This is one of those good news-bad news scenarios.

> **Good news:** *Our detail pages are showing up in organic search engine results for searches on the items we sell! Free traffic!*

> **Bad news:** *As landing pages, our detail pages leave a lot to be desired. They don't introduce our company well, they assume visitors who arrive there don't have any questions, they're kind of ugly and they don't even show our free shipping offer. How the heck did that happen?*

Plenty of companies don't have the resources to develop separate landing pages, so they send advertising traffic to their detail pages. These long-suffering pages then serve as the point of sale for visitors arriving via other site pages, as well as landing pages for organic and paid search campaigns.

While not ideal, this approach can still be reasonably successful if the product page is carefully crafted. Once again, as with many other site pages, even small changes can yield substantial improvements.

They tend to become cluttered

Perhaps it's because low-cost, templatized e-commerce platforms have become so common, but many of the detail pages we see are loaded down with so much extraneous junk we can barely find the offer. Navigation and banner ads yammer their way across the top and down the sides. Modules are strewn willy-nilly in any available space, first demanding then fragmenting attention:

Many of the detail pages we see are loaded down with so much extraneous junk we can barely find the offer.

Special Offers!   **E-mail Me to a Friend!**   **Write a Review!**

Today's Weather!   **Categories!**   **Funny Random Cat Photo!**

Animated Ads for Other Companies!   **Customer Login!**

And somewhere in the middle, gasping for breath amidst the chaos is the product. Not by itself, however. From below, it's hemmed in by Related Items, Reviews, Enlarged Images, More Details, and so forth ad infinitum.

There's nothing wrong with providing lots of information. There's not even anything wrong with adding other promotions to your detail page. But the "how" and "where" should be as carefully considered as the "what." Including any module on the page without thinking about its placement isn't good enough, not if you're serious about conversion.

A modular approach to detail page design places a multitude of equally-weighted action items on your page, all competing with the Add to Cart button for your visitor's attention. Which will win? More importantly: which do you *want* to win?

They are judged by a single image

More than any other page on your site, the success of your detail page can be made or broken by a single image—the *hero image* representing the offering. And while using a professional, high-quality image in this all-important spot seems like an obvious choice, we've encountered all kinds of excuses from clients for not having them.

For instance, there's

- The **A Picture's a Picture** excuse. Meaning as long as there's an image on the page, its quality doesn't matter.

- Then there's the **But I Have a Camera** excuse. Yes, if you're on a tight budget imagery is a tempting place to cut corners. Professional photography or illustration can be expensive and time consuming, so businesses often do it themselves.

- Last but not least, the **We Have a Great "Coming Soon" Image** excuse. Sorry, but not even the most attractive "No Image" place-holder can be as accurate and effective as the correct image.

The net result of these excuses? Millions of unattractive, unclear images that confuse, deter, or downright repel visitors instead of adding value to the detail page.

And, as if starting with a low-quality image weren't enough, many sites rub salt in the wound by scaling down the original image's size to fit into a too-small space. This renders the image as fuzzy and unattractive as a stray dog in need of a bath. What a way to create desire for your offering!

Hero image:

An image of the product or offering. Typically this image is the focal point of an ad or product information sheet.

Detail Page Design Guidelines

Focus attention: clearly define the detail display area

The focus of a detail page is the offering itself. Visitors want information about the item, and they want it quickly. Persistent site elements like navigation and advertising can confuse the focus of the detail page, making it more difficult for visitors to scan it quickly. To avoid this confusion, use space and/or design elements to clearly separate the detail display area from other site elements.

bose.com

This detail page uses a dark blue bar and white space to separate the detail display area from the top navigation and right-column links. The right-column area is relatively subdued, so it does not present too much of a distraction.

tigerdirect.com

This detail page does its best to separate the display area from the other page elements, but many different items battle for the visitor's attention here. The right-column advertisement and busy navigation headers are all distracting elements.

Use clear, professional images or rich media

This point can't be overemphasized for the detail page: use sharp, professional images. And, when necessary, use *rich media* like a video tour or animated Flash demo.

When should you use a video or animation instead of a still shot? When it makes your offer easier for visitors to understand without leaving the page. When, for instance, a single photo can't show all of the item's capabilities or features. If you show friends or colleagues a photo of your offer and they respond with a head-scratching "Huh?" then it's probably time for some rich media.

Rich media:

Content or information that consists of any combination of graphics, audio, video, and animation.

techsmith.com

This detail page includes an animated demo of SnagIt's abilities. The animation is paused on a shot of the product box, so visitors who are ready to buy don't have to wait. Those interested in more information can learn more right away, without leaving the page.

thinktankphoto.com

This detail page for an unusual camera backpack includes an animated slideshow displaying the backpack in various stages of use. A single image would not convey the features that differentiate this product from competitors.

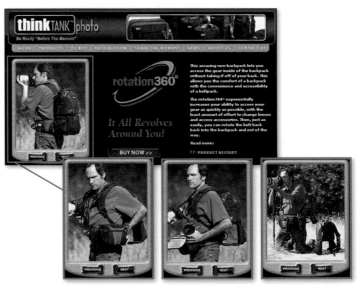

Consider showing the item in context

Some items are easier to understand and connect to when shown in context. In this case context means the item is displayed in its expected environment or while being experienced, used, or worn. Clothing is a common example. Visitors are more likely to understand how a jacket really looks when it's displayed on a model rather than on a flat surface.

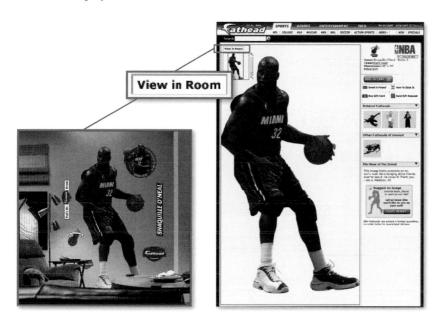

fathead.com

In addition to showing a large photo of the product—a life-size vinyl image—a View In Room button lets visitors see it in context, placed on a wall. This not only helps explain the product, it encourages prospective customers to imagine the item on their own walls.

brookstone.com

The photo for this product shows the flashlight being held and used, which distinguishes its use and benefits over other flashlights. It also provides a sense of scale that is easily lost when a plain background is used.

If it's a service, show the process or result

It's not always easy to communicate service offerings with images. How, for instance, does one photograph a home loan, investment advice, or piano lessons? One way is to show the service in process or show the result of the service.

Your choice of approach depends on the type of service. Experiential services such as travel, skill training, or entertainment are often better characterized by a photo or illustration from a high point in the experience process.

If the process isn't the most attractive part of the service, show the result. Dentists, for example, wisely use photos of happy people with great smiles, rather than open-mouthed, technical photos of dentistry in progress. Tile contractors, mortgage brokers, and career counselors are other examples of services whose processes are messy, confusing, or just not good representations of the service.

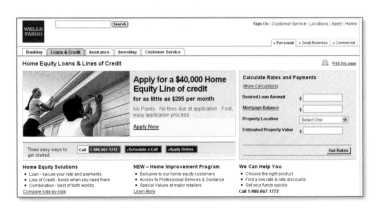

Cover all the important angles

Visitors can't touch or walk around your online item (at least, not yet), but they still want to know what the back looks like. And the sides, stitching, lining, brand, and anything else that's important. Providing these views keeps visitors on the detail page and answers questions about the item.

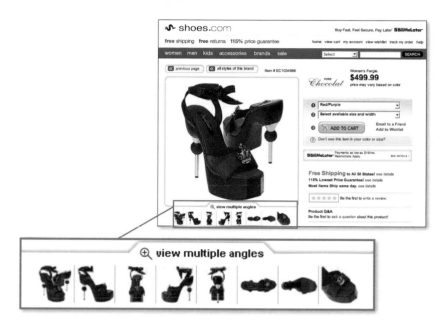

shoes.com

Each detail page on this site offers multiple views of the shoes. Mousing over the thumbnail images changes the main image to provide views from a variety of angles.

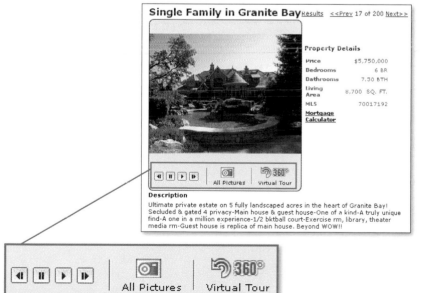

real estate site

Real estate detail pages usually include multiple photographs of the property, as well as a 360° video tour. In fact, it's hard to imagine trying to sell a property these days without providing this additional imagery.

Have a clear, descriptive heading

A clear, descriptive, easy-to-see heading reassures visitors they're on the right page. Without a strong heading, fast-moving visitors may assume they're in the wrong place and leave without really seeing the offer.

Prioritize and list the most important benefits and features

Visitors to a detail page want to understand the offering quickly. Help them out with a clear listing of the item's features and/or benefits. The trick is to choose the most important ones, so the visitor isn't overwhelmed with irrelevant information. How to choose, you might ask?

A feature or benefit is important to the detail page's conversion if...

- **Visitors care about it.** For example, roundness is a feature of a movie DVD, but nobody cares about it. Of much greater interest and relevance is special content such as features and interviews.

- **It differentiates the item** from others on your site or competitors' sites. Differentiators can be as simple as color, size, location, dates, or, as in the following examples, altitude.

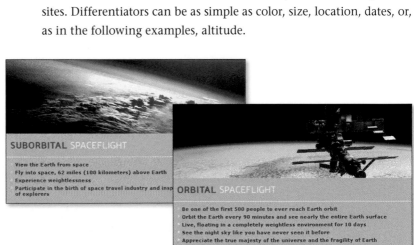

Include related items that enhance the offer

Adding related "you may also like" or optional accessory items to the detail page can increase the appeal of the offer. Make sure the selected additions are relevant and placed carefully. As with other design elements, related items can either enhance or distract from the main offer.

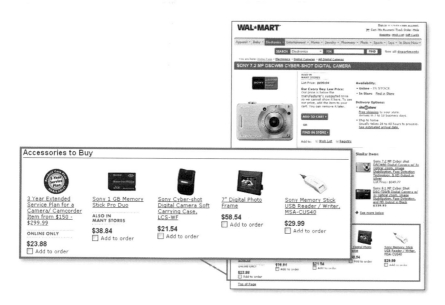

walmart.com

This detail page not only includes accessories appropriate to the item being offered but also allows a visitor to add them to an order right there. This makes it easier to buy additional items and keeps the visitor on the page, focused on the item at hand.

Make special offers obvious and contextual

There's a lot of free stuff available on the web, so visitors look for it—even expect it. When used properly promotional offers such as free shipping, special "web-only" prices, and free initial consultations help visitors think more kindly of a site and the organization behind it.

Visitors may expect special deals, but if they don't see them they'll assume you don't offer them. How do you make sure they get the message?

- **Place the offer contextually**. This means to place it near the item it applies to. Don't assume visitors will see your Free Shipping offer if it's plunked down in the middle of five other promotions in the right-hand column. Put it near the price, the item photo, or in another prominent spot in the detail display area to help ensure it's seen.

- **Make it stand out from other detail elements.** Use white space, a contrasting color, a graphic treatment, or all three.

- **State the offer clearly.** A special deal may make the sale, so it's no time to be subtle. Be descriptive and obvious with the offer's phrasing so hurried visitors grasp its meaning quickly.

Don't assume visitors will see your Free Shipping offer if it's plunked down in the middle of five other promotions in the right-hand column.

- **Keep legalese to a minimum.** If you have overzealous attorneys who insist on including disclaimers on all special offers, don't let the additional text overwhelm the offer itself. Instead, reference it with an asterisk and footnote whenever possible.

target.com

Can you find the free shipping offer on this page? Despite a very clean design on this detail page, visitors tend to miss the free shipping element (it's in red text, just above the item title). Using a graphical treatment or a contrasting color would help it stand out more effectively.

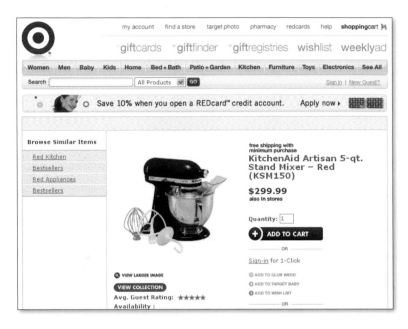

Use the description to make a connection

Anyone can describe a chair. Describing it so vividly the reader can see and feel it with their eyes closed, however, is an art. A well-crafted description is a powerful tool to put in your conversion tool belt. It pulls visitors in and connects them with the offer. It adds color and interest to the offer, making it more memorable. Will everyone read descriptions? No. But for those who do, the right words at the right time can make all the difference.

odwalla.com

The descriptions on this site make the products sound luscious—mission accomplished!

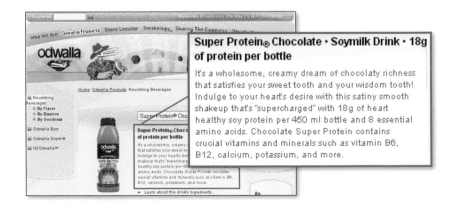

Provide social feedback information

Let's face it, people are social creatures. We like to know what other people think, and whether we realize it or not we're influenced by their opinions.

Social feedback information can be a powerful addition to a product page. It provides answers from a third party perceived to be objective. The addition of a download counter, for instance, immediately answers one question for visitors: has anyone else tried this item? Other types of social feedback include the following:

- Customer ratings
- Number of downloads
- Number of viewings
- Customer reviews

Social feedback:

Responses to or reviews of a product or service which are provided by site visitors, then compiled and displayed to other visitors.

bluenile.com

These jewelry detail pages include a summarized customer rating for the item and a link to view more customer feedback.

download.com

In addition to an Editor's Rating, these detail pages provide two types of social feedback—an average user rating and a count of the total number of downloads.

Make option selection easy and available

Option selection is where many visitors stumble or fall. If options are placed in an odd location on the page or displayed in an unclear manner, visitors can miss them entirely. Sometimes option names are unclear (exactly what color is "arctic ice," anyway?), or the thumbnail image doesn't provide enough detail. Or there's no larger view of each option, forcing visitors to use their imaginations. In sum, options can leave visitors uncertain about their choices and hesitant to take the next action, none of which helps a detail page's conversion rate.

A few general guidelines will help smooth this portion of the detail page's process:

- Place the options along the visual path between the main image and the action area.

- Keep the presentation clean and clear.

- Don't count on a tiny thumbnail to sell an option. If the option impacts the item's appearance or operation, be sure to provide a larger image of the item with each option applied. Don't make visitors guess.

- If there are multiple, interrelated options, make them dynamic so it's clear what combinations are available.

gap.com

On this detail page, the size and color options are clear, easy to see, and placed along the natural visual flow between the image and the Add to Bag button. Mousing over the color options puts the main image in the corresponding color. Mousing over or selecting any of the options, including waist size and length, highlights which other options are available in combination with the selected option.

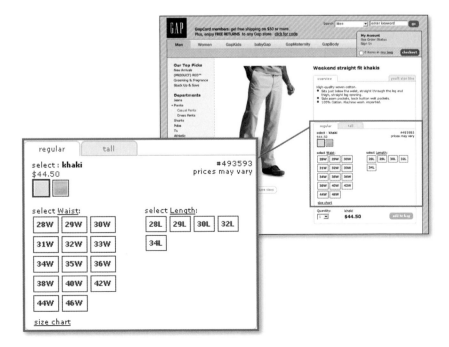

Provide availability information

Another factor influencing conversions is availability. The detail page is the right place to make this clear. Not in the shopping cart, and certainly not after the visitor has gone through the checkout process! A visitor who purchases an item only to find out it's on back-order for six weeks is going to be very unhappy with the offending company.

There are several ways to provide availability information. Some sites tie inventory systems to an availability counter. This is probably overkill for most situations, unless the item is in limited supply or large bulk orders are anticipated. Most visitors just want reassurance that their purchase won't be delayed.

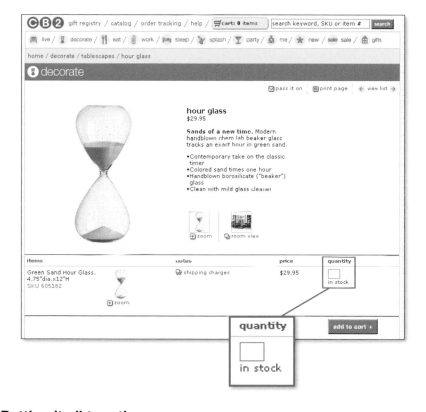

cb2.com

This detail page offers clear availability information, contextually placed next to the quantity field.

Putting it all together

Once again we've examined many page elements that have a considerable impact on page performance. So many, in fact, that it would be quite difficult to reliably test all possible combinations in an A/B test. How can you quickly tell which combination of elements provides the best performance? By using a technique called *multivariate testing*.

Multivariate testing:

An automated technique used to compare and measure the performance of one or more web page components.

Stop reading and try this...

FEATURED TECHNIQUE: Multivariate Testing

Multivariate testing may be thought of as automatically performing multiple A/B tests. In its simplest form, one important page component, such as the product image, is "tagged" with identifying code. Several alternate versions of the component are then created and kept ready for testing.

Each time a visitor arrives at the page, the automated system selects one of the component variations to display. The system tracks how well each variation performs based on what action visitors take, identifying over time which variation is most effective. For instance, if more visitors click the "Add to Cart" button when Image Variation #1 is used, that one would be deemed most effective.

Which image and heading combination will motivate the most conversions? Multivariate testing can tell you.

This simple example only scratches the surface of the possibilities. Multivariate testing is perfect for testing many different combinations of multiple elements at once. Not only is this a time-saver, it can be a money-saver as well, and with careful planning can be used on almost any page type. If your project is complex, consider having a professional set up and run the test for you.

Learn more:

Google Website Optimizer. A free service, but does require some technical expertise.

http://services.google.com/websiteoptimizer

Others. A number of companies provide multivariate testing services, and will help you design and run simple and complex tests. Search for "multivariate testing" on any search engine to locate a vendor.

Summary

The detail page plays a central role in determining your site's success. The more attractive, intuitive, and helpful your detail page is, the more likely it will outperform the competition.

But wait! Your visitors have put an item into the shopping cart, but they haven't purchased it yet. To do that, they'll probably have to fill out a few forms. Which is exactly what we'll look at next.

chapter 8

chapter 8

forms

*"Why, a four-year-old child could understand this.
Run out and find me a four-year-old child. I can't make heads
or tails of it."*

— *Groucho Marx, Duck Soup*

Forms are a way of life on the web. They're on shopping
sites, banking sites, social networking sites, and horoscope
sites. They can be as simple as a humble login form or as
critical and far-reaching as a financial account management form.

Organizations love forms. Forms put the burden of information gathering on
the visitor, thereby saving the organization time and customer service costs.
Visitors, however, aren't so enamored with forms, generally viewing them
with emotions running the unhappy gamut from boredom to impatience.

Why is this? One reason is that forms ask visitors to do difficult things, like
give up personal information, read fine print, look for documents, and
remember passwords. All the while keeping an eye out for phishers, identity
thieves, and e-mail abusers.

Another reason is that forms are fundamentally boring for visitors. Forms
don't sing, dance, or research potential stock investments; they're the
means to an end, not the end itself. The fun, rewarding stuff that visitors
want usually comes after a form is completed and submitted.

Since forms are crucial to many online processes, making them more
appealing and easier to use results in widespread benefits that cascade
through to other portions of a site. If forms are the road by which potential

leads and customers reach you, then smoothing out the potholes makes a world of difference to the journey.

Typical Form Goals

A form's primary goal is to be filled out and submitted, and this basic goal supports other larger purposes or processes. For example:

Form Goal	Example
Collect marketing information	A newsletter sign-up form
Guide visitors through a process	A service selection wizard
Enable a transaction	A form to transfer funds from one account to another
Communicate	A contact or feedback form
Verify identity	An account login form
Manage customer support requests	A trouble ticket form

Visitor Questions

Visitors have two types of questions about forms: those asked when arriving at a form and those asked while filling one out.

Arrival questions

When visitors arrive at a form, their questions are about appearance, reasonableness of the information requests, and security. Visitors attempt to answer these questions with a few quick glances.

- Where do I start?
- Does it look easy?
- Will it take a long time?
- Are there a lot of steps in the process?
- Is the outcome worth the effort?
- Is this page secure? Is my browser "lock" icon visible?
- Does it ask for a reasonable amount of information?

Process questions

As a visitor fills out the form, questions about privacy, clarity, and process arise. A form page should proactively provide information that answers these questions.

Some forms, of course, are complex and extend across several web pages. After the first few form fields, visitors tend to get into a form-filling "groove" and don't question each separate step in the process as closely as they did the first step. They can still be derailed by poor form design or unanswered questions, though.

- Are the questions reasonable? Do they fit the situation?
- Is my information secure and private? How private?
- I don't understand this question; is there an explanation?
- I'm not comfortable filling out the form online; is there another way?
- I'm having trouble with the form; how do I get help?
- What happens when I click the Submit button?
- How much more do I have to go?

Key Metrics for Forms

There's one form metric that's more important than any other:

- **Percentage of form submissions.** The percentage of visitors to a particular form page who successfully complete and submit the form on that page.

Example:

During August 1,000 unique visitors reach Form Page A. During the same period, web analytics show 370 unique clicks on the Submit button on Form Page A. The conversion rate for this form is

$$370 / 1,000 = 37\%.$$

Considerations

If a form is segmented across several pages, look at the submission percentage for each individual step. Visitors may breeze through some parts of your form and abandon or balk at others. In the Checkout Process chapter we take a closer look at using analytics to learn which parts of a process are problematic.

Unique Issues for Forms

Forms start out at a disadvantage to other web pages and are seldom welcomed with joy. This can be partly explained by examining the issues forms are prone to, including:

They look difficult

The elements of a form are not very friendly even when taken individually: all those short little boxes to type in, the rigid rows that resemble a to-do list, the tiny black letters, the authoritative tone. Put them all together, and the result is often a complex-looking combination. The more difficult the form looks, the stronger the incentive visitors need to fill it out.

They get greedy

Any form that includes fields unnecessary for its main purpose is a greedy form.

Any form that includes fields unnecessary for its main purpose is a greedy form. In our experience, forms will become greedy unless they're diligently controlled. A form may start out slim and unassuming with four tidy little fields. Then someone in Sales notices the form isn't asking for a fax number, or favorite color, or some other piece of remotely useful information, and the runaway bloat begins.

We're not saying a short form is best in every situation or for every company. But most forms we've seen include extraneous "nice to have" fields that could be eliminated or condensed with no loss of information quality.

They take too long to get to the point

Many online forms are divided across multiple consecutive web pages. The visitor completes a form on the first page, clicks Submit, waits for the next page to load, and so forth. From the visitor's perspective this is a disjointed, pothole-ridden experience. From an organization's perspective, each pause introduces a possible abandonment point.

In the past, there were programming and cost reasons for this approach. These days, however, newer programming approaches and technologies, like Ajax and Flash, offer ways to provide a smoother, faster, more seamless visitor experience.

They break

Anyone who's filled out a lot of forms has had at least one of them stop functioning at a critical juncture—usually after laboriously entering reams of information. Why don't forms always work perfectly? Partly because there are so many different elements that have to function properly. Many of these elements, like the power supply, server connection cables, or the performance of a visitor's ISP, are outside an organization's control. But others, like poor code, are entirely avoidable.

Form Design Guidelines

The phrase "form design" may seem like an oxymoron to designers. Forms are, after all, the public-works buildings of the web. They're meant to be functional and utilitarian, not frilly and entertaining.

Designing forms is indeed more about problem solving than pure artistic creativity. The problem in this case is how to create a utilitarian form interface that is as inviting, clear, and easy as possible for the visitor to complete.

Focus attention on the form area

The sooner you can focus a visitor's attention on the form, the sooner they'll know what to do and where to start. This guideline is as important for subsequent forms in a multi-step process as it is for the initial form in the process.

The phrase "form design" may seem like an oxymoron to many designers. Forms are, after all, the public works buildings of the web.

netquote.com

This single-field landing page form employs several tactics to focus attention—a border around the form area, an eye-catching graphic next to the form, and a pointing person.

Forms can appeal to the eye even though they're basically utilitarian. There are a number of ways to make forms stand out on a page, such as

- A light background color behind the form (but make sure the text is still easy to read)

- A border around the form

- Colored field boxes

- Arrows

marsrover.nasa.gov

This form allowing educators to request a free Mars poster uses background color to distinguish the form area from the rest of the page.

ucop.edu

A border and shaded areas across the top and bottom help focus attention on this application form for the University of California.

Use a clean, simple layout

To reduce the perception of a form being difficult or complex, simplify and clean up the form layout.

What makes a form look simple and clean?

- **White space.** Leave enough empty space—whatever the color— around the form and between the form rows. This improves legibility and scannability.

- **Removal of all extraneous elements.** Everything in, on, and around a form should contribute to its completion and submission.

- **Clear label-field association.** There is such a thing as too much space, especially when it's between a field and its label. Too much space here makes visitors try to track horizontally across a blank area hoping to end up at the correct field. Strongly associate the field with the label by positioning them closely together.

- **Legible text.** Make sure the form text doesn't send visitors diving for their reading glasses. Tiny, low-contrast text (like pale gray on a white background) is difficult to read on a computer monitor. The text used for form field labels and inside the fields themselves should be high-contrast, uncomplicated typography that's easy to read.

Make sure the form text doesn't send visitors diving for their reading glasses.

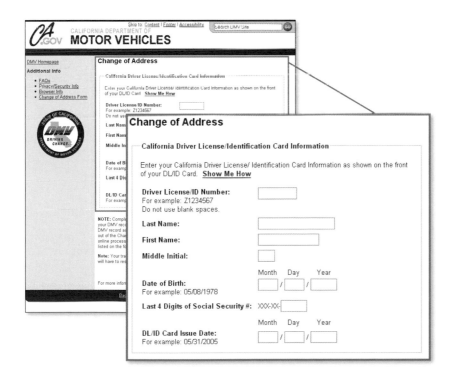

dmv.ca.gov

We were pleasantly surprised to find forms with clean, simple layouts on the California DMV site.

This change of address form illustrates the guidelines we discuss here, especially legible text, good use of white space, and use of left-aligned text and fields to improve scannability.

- **Left-aligned text and fields.** Visitors look to the left to locate the beginning of a text line. Right-aligned text makes it more difficult to locate the beginning of each line, increasing the apparent complexity of the form. Left-aligned fields also help visually organize the layout for easier, faster scanning.

Right-aligned text:

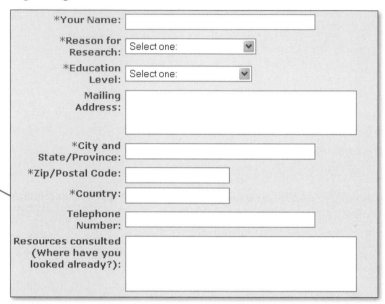

Text alignment

A form with left-aligned text will appear simpler and easier than one with right-aligned text.

In this right-aligned text example, notice how each line of text begins at a different horizontal point. More eye motion is required to scan and read these labels.

Left-aligned text:

Notice how a consistent beginning point for all lines of text makes it easier to scan straight down the field labels.

Be ruthless: remove unnecessary fields

Most forms ask for more than is absolutely necessary, and as a general prin-
ciple the more fields a form has, the less its chance of completion. That said,
however, a form submission is useful and valuable only if it contains a suf-
ficient amount of qualifying information. There are always indispensable
fields. For example, a company might need a ZIP code to refer visitors to the
correct service area or an e-mail address to enable a newsletter subscription.
The challenge is to strike a balance between qualifying visitors and boost-
ing conversions. We believe a form is ready for prime time only when every
field can be rigorously defended as absolutely necessary.

Before:

After:

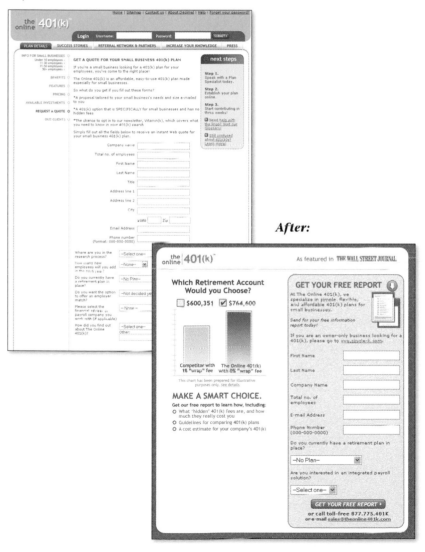

theonline401k.com

*The original landing
page included a long,
complicated-looking form
with no fewer than 21
fields.*

*We reduced the form field
count from 21 to 8, with
no reported impact on
lead quality. Fewer fields,
combined with the new
form design and updated
messaging, yielded a 200%
conversion increase.*

Overcome hesitation with benefits

Remind visitors of the benefits they'll receive by filling out a form. Remember, you may not have their complete and undivided attention during their visit to your site. They may be sidetracked by a ringing phone, an IM, or any number of distractions in their environment. The clearer the benefits, the easier it is for visitors to get started.

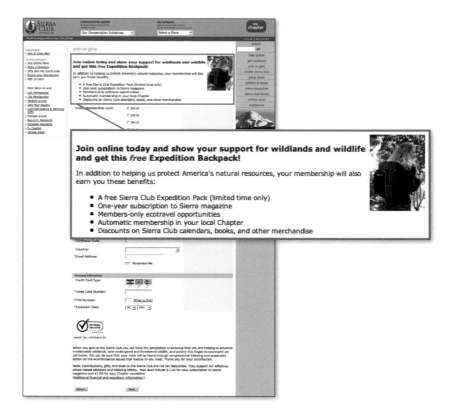

sierraclub.org

The Sierra Club's membership/donation page provides a list of benefits, complete with a picture of the free backpack.

Use clear, descriptive field labels

Writing descriptive, effective field labels is an art in itself. Certainly, the typical ones are easy enough: First Name, Last Name, Address, and so forth. But using a generic label can cause misunderstandings.

For example, depending on the context, the label Username could be either a request for an existing username or a directive to create a new username for a new account. We've seen visitors stumble over this distinction by thinking they were being asked to remember a username that didn't yet exist.

Consider using active verbs

When there is room for doubt or misinterpretation, using active verbs in the label can help clarify and guide the process. Here are a few examples:

Passive Labels	Active Labels
Country / Region	Select the country or region where you live
Language	Choose your language preference
Password	Create an account password
Domain name	Enter your current domain name

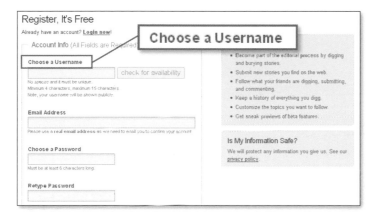

digg.com

The field labels on this registration form use active verbs to sidestep potential confusion. For instance, the verb "choose" clarifies the Username and Password labels.

Consider using sentence completion

Another alternative is to tie the label and field together into a sentence. The field label begins the phrase, and the field options "fill in the blank."

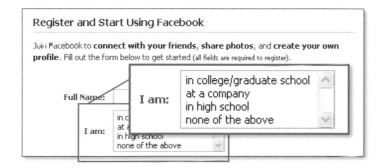

facebook.com

This registration form uses a creative approach to clarify a field label. Rather than a potentially confusing descriptor, like Status or Employment/ School, the label begins a sentence and the field options complete it.

Consider using a complete question

In some cases using a complete question is the clearest way to label a form field:

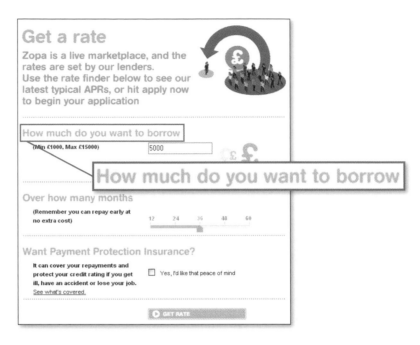

Provide help and contextual answers

Filling out a form can be a lonely experience. There's the visitor, sitting at the kitchen table with a laptop trying to fill out a complicated form with no help from anyone except a ten-year-old neighbor kid. What if questions come up? What if the form asks for something odd or unfamiliar?

Many questions are answered best with contextual information, meaning the answer is placed near the area or item that triggers the question.

Of course, forms would quickly become messy and chaotic if explanatory text was next to every field. One solution is to provide the contextual information in a linked pop-up window or layer. This shifts the explanation off the surface of the form, leaving it clean and simple looking while offering assistance when and where it's needed.

Some visitors will want the reassurance of human interaction. Provide a phone number or a live chat feature to fill this need.

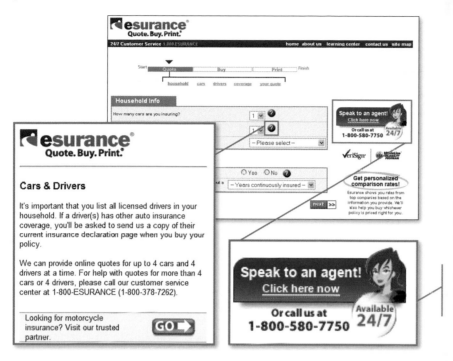

esurance.com

This form provides contextual information via pop-up windows linked from a question-mark button. This provides a detailed answer without cluttering up the form. Notice that buttons are placed contextually—that is, close to the fields—so there's no doubt about the relationship.

Phone and chat options are also available for visitors with questions.

Allow estimated answers

Many forms ask for information that's not immediately handy. Requiring an exact, correct answer at this point is like telling the visitor "Quit now, it's not going to get any easier!" Whenever possible, ask for an estimated, rather than exact, answer and make it clear when a best guess is acceptable.

lowermybills.com

This mortgage loan application form provides extra reassurance that an estimated entry is acceptable.

Prefill as many fields as possible

Once a visitor begins to fill out a form, it's in everyone's best interest for the process to go quickly. If some of your form questions have common answers, make them the defaults for those fields. For example, if you know the significant majority of your visitors are from the United States, make the Country field default to United States.

At minimum, place the most common selections at the top of any long list of options, and repeat them in the longer, full list if needed. This reduces the number of clicks and mouse movements visitors have to make in order to complete the form. There, that's much easier!

Clearly indicate the steps or time involved

Think of the last time you got driving directions from a friend or an online map site. Isn't it reassuring to know approximately how long it will take to get to your destination? Visitors facing a multi-page form process feel the same way. They'd like to know in advance what kind of time commitment they're getting into.

If you have a lengthy form process, it may be tempting to obscure the fact by not providing any indicators. This can backfire. Many experienced visitors won't even start a form without some advance information. Other visitors willingly start a form and slog on for one or two pages, then grow weary and drop out if they can't get a sense for how much longer the form will take to complete.

livestrong.org

This donation form includes a graphic element indicating how many steps there are in the process and what to expect at each step.

Provide security and privacy reassurance

With the growth of identity theft, phishing, e-mail spam, and other security concerns, reassuring your visitors about the security and privacy of their information is increasingly important.

Of course, it's not enough merely to reassure visitors. Behind the scenes, organizations must comply with credit card company requirements and government regulations about the handling and storage of customer information. And while visitors may not be aware of these efforts, they will look for evidence of trustworthiness.

Many visitors will automatically look for the "lock" icon on their web browser to check whether a form is using a secure connection, so make sure this is present for forms that ask for personal information.

Other visitors will look for, or at least notice and be reassured by, privacy and security icons. These can include a secure certificate icon or a seal from a privacy verification company such as TRUSTe. Examples of secure certificate and privacy verification icons include:

Finally, questions of privacy and security arise when a specific request is made for sensitive information—such as an e-mail address, credit card number, or social security number. Place a brief, clear summary of your privacy and security policy near this request.

marketingsherpa.com

This purchase form includes a reassurance about information safety and security, contextually placed near the payment information fields.

Putting it all together

Because forms are interactive, it can be difficult to pinpoint form problems without watching visitors use them. Which is where *informal usability testing* can be very helpful.

It's become an open secret among web professionals that usability testing doesn't have to be a formal, expensive undertaking to be beneficial. While there is much value in large-scale, rigorous testing, it can be pricey and time-consuming. Informal usability testing will quickly uncover many qualitative interaction issues that could otherwise be missed.

Informal usability testing:

An approach to usability testing that emphasizes discovery of major design and interactivity problems in any type of interface. Typically used in earlier stages of design and development.

FEATURED TECHNIQUE:
Informal Usability Testing

What does an informal usability test look like? It can be as simple as asking a few friends and colleagues to try out your site while you observe and document their reactions. To get the most out of an informal test, do the following:

- **Test early and often**. The earlier you conduct user testing in your site update or development process, the easier and less expensive it is to make needed changes. For instance, getting feedback on concept sketches or using a method called *paper prototyping* to test a layout or interactive process will provide valuable insights before hours of design and development have been committed to the project.

- **Plan the scope of your test in advance**. Decide what task, page, or element you want feedback on, and limit your test to that.

- **Practice your test**. Plan how you'll record participant feedback, whether you'll need an assistant, where participants will sit, where you'll sit, what materials you'll need, how you'll begin the test, what you'll say, and what each step should be. Practice on coworkers or family members.

- **Select test participants** with characteristics similar to those of your site's audience.

- **Include at least five participants**. More participants will uncover more issues and provide more reliable results, but you'll gain valuable insights from as few as five.

- **Assure the participants that they aren't being tested or graded**. They're helping you to improve your site. Encourage them to think out loud and to be honest.

- **Avoid guiding or prompting the participants**. After describing the task to them, do not attempt to help them complete it if they stumble. Wait to see what they do on their own.

Paper prototyping:

A type of usability test that simulates a web interface using paper mockups. Paper prototyping is valuable for providing early insight into the usability of draft designs or processes.

- **Keep your language neutral and nonjudgmental**. If participants give suggestions or criticisms, thank them and assure them that their input is helpful.

- **Document feedback and observations** (for example, "Participant B did not see the sign-up link."). You may need an assistant to do this for you, while you administer the test.

- **Summarize your findings**. Note any repeated patterns or feedback, because these represent areas that warrant further study.

Learn more:

Usability Net.
  http://www.usabilitynet.org/tools/test&measure.htm
Usability.gov.
  http://www.usability.gov/refine/index.html
Others: Find other resources by searching for "how to run a usability test" on Google or another search engine.

Summary

Forms may not be the most welcome of web page elements, but they are crucial to the success of many web sites. Simple design updates can make them less painful for visitors and more effective for site conversion goals.

Next, we look at a common yet frequently confusing form-based feature, a veritable form jungle in which more than half of all prospective customers are lost: the checkout process.

chapter 9

checkout process

"I have enough money to last me the rest of my life, unless I buy something."

— Jackie Mason

The checkout process is one of the most widespread and familiar of all online processes. As such, it's had plenty of time to be studied, analyzed, and tweaked. It could be said the checkout process is so commonplace it's been perfected. Right?

Wrong. Improvements to the checkout process have been unevenly implemented across the web, and will take time to be widely distributed. Many commonly used shopping cart systems, for example, continue to incorporate outdated approaches to the checkout process, perpetuating mistakes or limitations from the early days of the web. The result? An average of 59.8% of all visitors entering a checkout process abandon it before completion.

Nowhere but on the web would this statistic be tolerated. Can you imagine a grocery store where 59% of customers abandoned their shopping carts, leaving them scattered around the store and piled up around the checkout counters? The store management would consider it an emergency of epic proportion! They would immediately fly in high-priced retail traffic flow advisors via Learjet to fix the problem. Online, amazingly, this level of failure is regularly tolerated.

This, despite the fact that once visitors start the checkout process they usually intend to complete it. Sure, some are shopping for entertainment and decide at the last minute they don't actually *need* a SpongeBob SquarePants

Can you imagine a grocery store where 59% of customers abandoned their shopping carts, leaving them scattered around the store and piled up around the checkout counters?

beach towel. Others are comparison-shopping and bail when they see a better offer, or are using the cart as a printable wish list. The majority, however, actively *want* to buy the contents of their shopping cart. All they need is a clear, simple path with no roadblocks.

Luckily for online shoppers, the future promises a much improved experience. As more organizations realize the potential impact on their ROI, they are responding with innovative techniques and technologies that create a smoother, friendlier, more reliable checkout process.

Typical Checkout Process Goals

The primary goal of the checkout process is to enable a financial transaction—one where the visitor hands over money or the promise of payment in exchange for an item or service. That's it!

Of course, this financial transaction can be for many different purposes, depending on the site and the offering. Here are a few examples:

Type of Site	Purpose for a Checkout Process
Charitable organization	Accept donations
E-commerce	Allow purchases
Investment newsletter	Set up recurring membership payments
Political campaign	Accept donations
Virtual world	Transform real money into its virtual equivalent

To achieve this primary goal a checkout process must successfully perform a number of sub-tasks, including but not limited to the following:

- Remember and display collected items upon request.
- Collect shipping or delivery information and validate it.
- Collect billing and payment information and validate it.
- Connect to a payment gateway and process or schedule a payment.

Visitor Questions

Visitors using a checkout process need reassurance, clear directions, and above all, the answers to a few questions:

Initial questions

- Where do I start? How do I check out?
- Do I have to register? I just want to buy something.
- What is my password? I can't even remember if I shopped here before!
- Am I still at the same store? Everything suddenly looks different.
- How long will this take?

Mid-process questions

- What does "Billing Address" mean, exactly?
- How much will shipping cost?
- What if I need to return it?
- Is this secure?
- Why do they want that particular information?
- I'm not comfortable filling out an online form. Is there another way?
- I'm having trouble with the form. How do I get help?

Payment questions

- What payment methods are accepted?
- What's a "card verification number"?
- What happens when I click the Submit button?

Completion questions

- Will I get a receipt?
- When will I receive my purchase?

Key Metrics for Checkout Processes

It's easy to oversimplify checkout process metrics by focusing only on the final step—a successful purchase—but this approach doesn't provide enough detail. After all, checkout processes are inherently complex. They often have a number of separate steps, including:

- Shopping cart review
- Login (if a returning customer)
- Registration (if new to the store)
- Billing address/shipping address
- Payment information
- Purchase review
- Confirmation

Phew! Doesn't it seem nearly miraculous that in 2006 there were $29.73 billion of successful online purchases* in the U.S. alone?

Amazement aside, any of those individual steps in a checkout process could be a conversion trouble spot. The way to pinpoint problems accurately is to track the conversion rate and dropoff rate at each and every step.

- **Conversion rate.** The percentage of visitors who proceed to the next step.
- **Dropoff rate.** The percentage of visitors who do NOT proceed to the next step.

Why do we look at *both* mirror opposite percentages? To improve clarity. For example, a 73% conversion rate might sound pretty darn good until you realize this means 27% of your customers—more than a quarter!—dropped off.

Example:

A look at the site log files reveals that 1,000 visitors viewed the Shopping Cart page last month:

Step	Visitor Count
Shopping Cart	1,000

A 73% conversion rate might sound pretty darn good until you realize this means 27% of your customers—more than a quarter!— dropped off.

*MarketingSherpa 2007 Ecommerce Data

So far, so good. But is the Shopping Cart page effectively moving visitors towards checkout? We won't know unless we count how many visitors arrived at the next step.

In this case, the next step is a Login page. Another look at the site log reveals that 950 unique visitors viewed the Login page last month:

Step	Visitor Count
Shopping Cart	1,000
Login	950

This means 950 of the original 1,000 visitors, or 95%, successfully proceeded from the Shopping Cart step to the Login step. 95%, then, is the Conversion Rate for the Shopping Cart step. Viewed from the "failure" point of view, 50 visitors, or 5%, did not complete the step. 5% is our Dropoff Rate for the Shopping Cart step.

Step	Visitor Count	Conversion Rate	Dropoff Rate
Shopping Cart	1,000	95%	5%
Login	950	(To be determined)	

See the "Featured Technique" section for an example analysis using an analytics package.

Unique Issues for Checkout Processes

It's not only individual steps that can present problems. There are other, more general issues associated with checkout processes.

They're burdened by the past

Like human dysfunctions, many irrational checkout characteristics are rooted in the past. At one time, it made sense to force every visitor to register or sign in before purchasing something. After all, that eased integration with order fulfillment systems, among other things. At one time, it also made sense to divide the purchase process into multiple pages, to accommodate slow internet connections.

Like human dysfunctions, many irrational checkout characteristics are rooted in the past.

Although they've outlived their original purpose and usefulness, these legacies continue to appear in—and bog down—many checkout processes.

They break

Checkout processes are built from code, just like other parts of a web site, and code can fail. So can database connections, payment gateway communications, and secure servers. Some of the more dramatic failures we've seen, though, are due to human error, like the time we examined a checkout process that literally had *no way* for a visitor to continue past the Shipping Address page. The Continue button had vanished, accidentally hidden behind an unclosed comment tag in the code.

Because checkout processes are crucial to many sites' success, their metrics require vigilant oversight to detect any unforeseen problems.

They're scary

Despite the growing familiarity and popularity of online commerce, many visitors harbor doubt about the process and fears about the security of personal information. As a Dilbert cartoon once eloquently illustrated, though people may hand over their physical credit cards to unknown waiters in restaurants, many feel uneasy purchasing online, even from a well-known organization.

It's not an entirely unreasonable apprehension. Education about online safety, in our opinion, has not kept pace with the growing sophistication of security threats. While more and more credit card companies and online stores are stepping up to provide "safe shopping" guarantees, rarely has the phrase "caveat emptor" (buyer beware) been as relevant as it is online today.

They put on masks

Speaking of scary, many sites surprise visitors with a third-party shopping cart that looks completely different from the rest of the site. What should visitors think about this? They hear rumors about online scams to steal credit card information, and suddenly they're in the web equivalent of a dark alley in a strange city, being asked to provide exactly that. There's nothing wrong with using a separate shopping cart system for a site, but too often the visual transition from one to the other is confusing.

Because checkout processes are crucial to many sites' success, their metrics require vigilant oversight to detect any unforeseen problems.

Visitors hear rumors about online scams to steal credit card information, and suddenly they're in the web equivalent of a dark alley in a strange city, being asked to provide exactly that.

Checkout Process Design Guidelines

Because a checkout process usually extends over several steps, any design effort needs to consider the entire flow and what effect a change to one step may have on the others. For example, a change to a button label means a change in visitor expectations for what comes next. Removing a registration step may require adding fields to other steps. Color changes to one step should be reflected across the process. And so forth.

So while considering which design guidelines would benefit your checkout process, also consider what other changes may need to be made as a result.

Apply basic form design guidelines

As we consider forms in the context of the checkout process, some key form guidelines bear review:

- **Remove unnecessary fields.** Make sure every form field is indispensable, not simply "nice to have."

- **Use a clean, simple layout.** Use appropriate space, alignment, and legible fonts.

- **Focus attention on the form area.** Use a light background color, border, or other design elements to distinguish the form area from the rest of the page.

- **Provide help and contextual answers.** Phone numbers, chat links, and linked popup windows with answers all help create a more informed and confident process.

- **Indicate process steps.** Let visitors know how many steps to expect and where they are in the process. More on this later.

- **Provide security reassurances.** Use icons and linked notices in strategic positions to reassure visitors. More on this later, as well.

Help visitors remember what's in the cart

Ever forget what you put in your shopping cart, or worry you clicked the wrong brand or color by accident? Wouldn't it be nice to be able to see what you selected, rather than trying to read cryptic item descriptions in tiny grey font?

Many carts make it difficult to see and double-check their contents, leaving visitors doubtful at a crucial decision point. Naturally they want to be certain of their *exact* selections before purchasing them!

The best way to reassure visitors? Include a thumbnail image of each item right in the cart. Next best? Make the item titles super clear, descriptive, and in a font large enough to read. Also include information about selected options such as color and size, and provide links back to each item so visitors can verify.

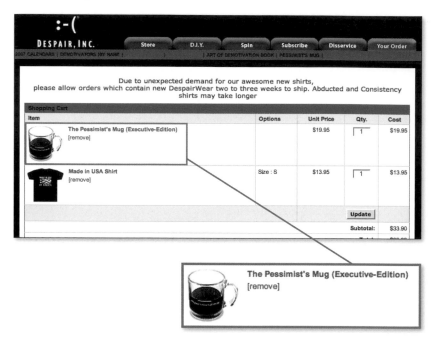

Prioritize those buttons

We discussed button design in the Landing Pages chapter, but let's examine special issues associated with the checkout process.

Oops! You meant to recalculate the cart total, but instead you deleted its contents! Sorry, you should've read the button labels more carefully.

Buttons play a key role during checkout, helping visitors update their carts, calculate shipping, and move from one step to the next. But what happens when all the buttons look exactly the same? Visitors have to read them to determine their importance and function. This is especially difficult for visitors when four, five, or more buttons are on the same page at once, identical except for their labels and function. Oops! You meant to recalculate the cart total, but instead you deleted its contents! Sorry, you should've read the button labels more carefully.

This lack of button prioritization is often present in templated e-commerce systems, illustrated by the following example:

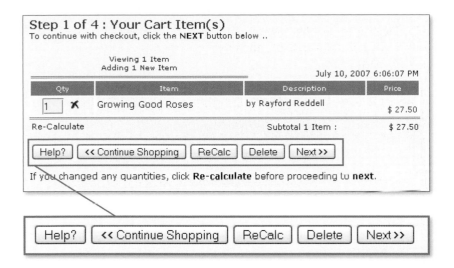

Gardening site

A sign of trouble ahead: buttons so unclear they require text explanations and instructions! This is a typical templated shopping cart, visually confusing, with no fewer than five equally-weighted buttons. There are no visual clues to help visitors tell which button is most important or what it does. The only distinguishing feature is the button label text, which forces visitors to read.

In contrast, the following example cart uses a variety of button styles and placements to indicate their priority and importance:

cduniverse.com

This shopping cart offers more possible actions than the previous example, but clearly prioritizes them with different placements and visual treatments.

The Continue Shopping action is de-emphasized—perhaps a bit too much—by appearing as a text link placed above the main cart area.

Notice the Complete Your Order button is the largest, most prominent button on the page and is intuitively placed at the lower right of the cart.

Prioritized buttons help guide visitors forward by indicating the relative importance of each available action. Placing them in expected, intuitive locations helps visitors find the action they need, when they need it.

Make the process steps clear

Regardless how many steps there are in the checkout process, visitors are more comfortable when they know what to expect. As we discussed in the Forms chapter, be sure to provide a step indicator showing what is coming up and where the visitor is located in the sequence. This is important for any process, but especially so during checkout.

bmgmusic.com

The checkout steps on this site are clearly indicated and numbered above the cart, and remain in place for each step of the process.

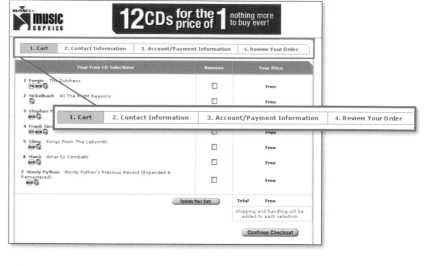

virgin-atlantic.com

The checkout process makes effective use of colored airplane icons to indicate progress. Although the steps are not numbered, visitors can see what lies ahead. A "Previous" link allows visitors to go back to earlier steps to make changes or corrections.

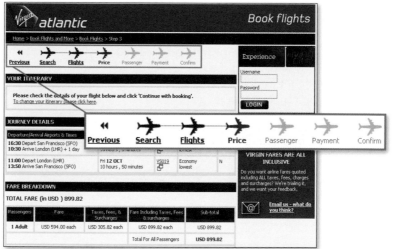

Make it easy to begin: don't require new visitors to register

The first thing many visitors see when they click the Checkout button is a Login/Registration page, and this is exactly where we typically see a large dropoff rate. Making registration a condition of purchase is counterintuitive, at least from the visitors' point of view. They know they have to provide their full shipping, billing, and payment information in order to complete their purchase—isn't that enough?

The solution is to eradicate this visitor roadblock. Instead of requiring account setup before proceeding with the checkout process, ask for account-specific information (such as a password) during the regular checkout flow.

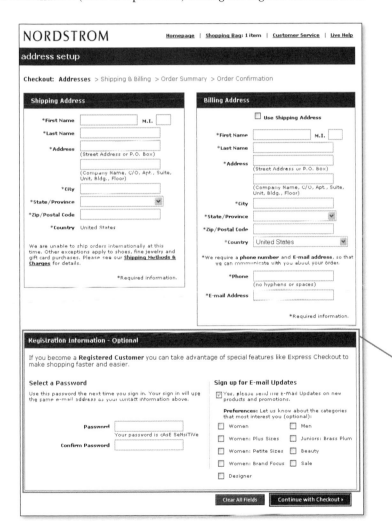

nordstrom.com

Nordstrom's approach avoids the initial hurdle of filling out a separate registration form, increasing the likelihood that visitors will complete their purchase.

For first-time visitors, this site integrates an optional registration into the first step of the checkout process.

Reduce the number of steps—or simplify them

Fewer steps in a process increase conversions, right? Typically, yes. With all other factors—such as visitor motivation—being equal, a short checkout process will convert at a higher rate than a long one. But it's not quite as simple as that. The clarity and flow of the steps, not their number, is what has the greatest effect on conversions. It only takes one unclear, poorly conceived step to make your conversion rate tank.

This is good news if you're stuck with an e-commerce platform that has a rigid, unalterable number of steps. By paying careful attention to the layout and design of each checkout step you can improve your conversion rate without changing platforms.

Example:

This online store undertook a design facelift to its checkout process that resulted in a 20% reduction in the cart abandonment rate, which translated into millions in increased annual revenues for the company. Changes were made only to design and layout. A few fields were moved or deleted, but the number and order of steps in the process remained the same.

Before:

After:

166

Before:

Old cart

Comments and Promotion Code fields appeared above four very similar-looking buttons, asking for information too soon and being unclear about the next step. The company had a free shipping offer, but it was not visible.

After:

New cart

The new cart removes the Comments field, introduces a process-step indicator at the top, and uses color, size and placement to indicate button priority and function. The Free Shipping notice is prominent in the left column.

Old review and payment info page

This page combined order review with fields for payment information. Confusingly, the billing address entered earlier was redisplayed with the new heading Credit Card Billing Address. No security notice or icons were on the page, and a big, scary-looking disclaimer hovers above the Purchase button.

Before:

Final Purchase Approval

home > final purchase approval

- Your purchase total is **$323.25.**
- Please enter your payment information then click the "PURCHASE" button below.

Item #	Name Attributes	Qty	Price Each	Your Price	Discount	Total
14875	Altus Fan Brushed Aluminum,36 Inches,Aluminum,75W Incandescent,Fan Speed and Light Control	1	$300.00	$300.00	$0.00	$300.00

Sub-Total:	$300.00
Shipping:	Ground - Free ▾
Tax:	$23.25
TOTAL:	$323.25

Shipping Information

Edit your shipping information

Payment Information

First Name: _____   Last Name: _____

Card Number: _____

Type: VISA ▾

Expires: Oct ▾ 2005 ▾

Enter the Card ID below:

American Express: 4 digits on front of card

Visa and Mastercard: last 3 digits on back of card

Card ID: _____

Credit Card Billing Address

Company: _____

Street: _____

Apartment: _____

City: _____

State: California ▾

ZIP Code: _____

Country: United States ▾

Phone: _____

E-mail: _____

Addtional Information

Returns accepted for regularly-priced items within 30 days provided that the product has not been installed, has not been damaged in any way, and is in its complete and original packaging suitable for resale. No returns of light bulbs, lamps shades, customized products, sale products, or items that have been cut or installed. Cost of any free shipping extended will be deducted from refunds.

Restocking fee of $15% charged for returned items that are not defective. Damaged goods must be reported within 24 hours of receipt. A Returned Goods Authorization number must be provided before returns can be accepted. We reserve the right to cancel any order for items with inaccurate product or pricing information.

PURCHASE

After:

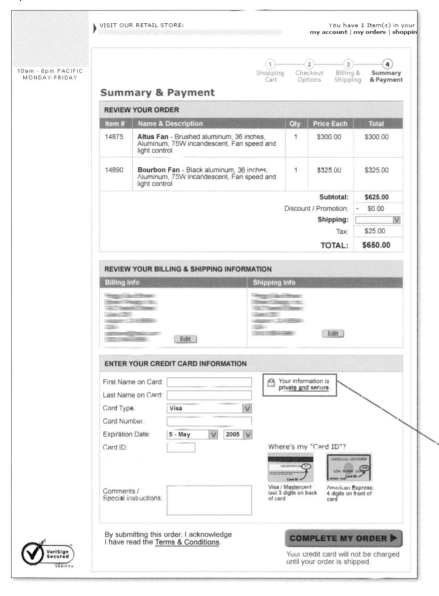

New review and payment info page

Because there are three separate tasks—Review Order, Review Billing & Shipping Information, and Enter Credit Card Information—on the page, the new page uses active verbs in the headings to help guide visitors through.

The repeated Billing Address fields are removed, and the Comments field previously located on the Cart page is moved here.

A security notice with a link to the company's policy is added next to the Credit Card fields.

Reduce to a single step

If you have the flexibility to make major changes to your checkout process, then consider consolidating all the normally separate steps onto a single scrollable page. Modern single-step checkouts often include some Ajax functionality to handle secondary interactions such as account logins and shipping address selection. The streamlined, simplified process flow typically results in an improved checkout completion rate.

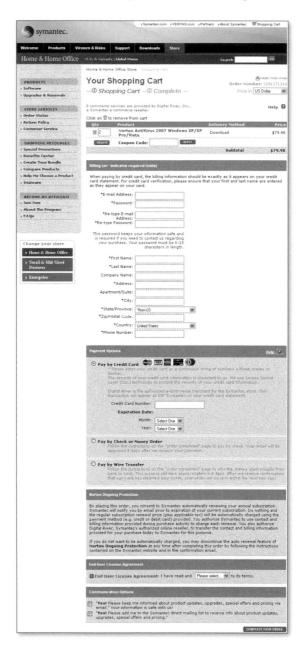

Provide security and privacy reassurances

It's important to provide reassurances whenever visitors are asked for personal information. This is especially true of a checkout process, where credit card or other payment information is requested.

In our experience, while only a small percentage of visitors click on security or privacy links to check a certificate or read a company's policy statement, nearly all visitors notice the presence—or absence—of these reassurances. A checkout process without some sort of security and privacy notification is viewed with doubt, and is more likely to be abandoned than one with credible notices in place.

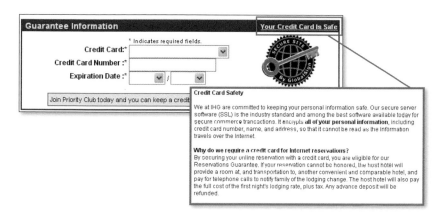

ichotelsgroup.com

This registration form includes a secure services icon and a reassurance (Your Credit Card Is Safe) linked to a more detailed security statement.

Provide shipping and return policy information

One of the many online shopping concerns visitors have is whether they can return an item that's defective, damaged, or simply the wrong size. Reassure visitors by providing clear links to shipping and return policy information.

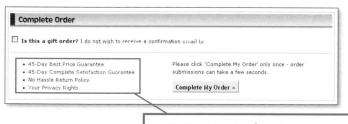

musiciansfriend.com

Contextually placed next to the final Complete My Order button are multiple reassuring links, including one to the return policy. This answers questions at a crucial point, helping smooth the process to a successful completion.

Stop reading and try this...

FEATURED TECHNIQUE: Metrics Analysis

While a metrics analysis is possible to do by looking at your log files, the process is *much* easier with a good analytics package. If you don't already have an analytics package we recommend trying one out as soon as possible. Installation can be as simple as adding a snippet of code to each page of your site and designating which pages constitute your checkout process.

On the next page is some sample output from Google Analytics. This is a visual representation of the performance of a complete checkout process over a specific time period, with each step identified by name. For each step, the number and percentage of visitors who proceeded, as well as the number who dropped off, are noted.

In this sample checkout process there are a number of problem points with high dropoff rates. Each dropoff reduces traffic to the next step, resulting in an overall conversion rate of only 16.38% for this checkout process. Let's take a closer look at a couple of the worst dropoff points (next page):

Learn more:

Google Analytics.
http://www.google.com/analytics

WebTrends.
http://www.webtrends.com

ClickTracks.
http://www.clicktracks.com

OneStat.
http://www.onestat.com

More.
*Search online for "web analytics" to see more analytics packages.
Most provide a free trial period.*

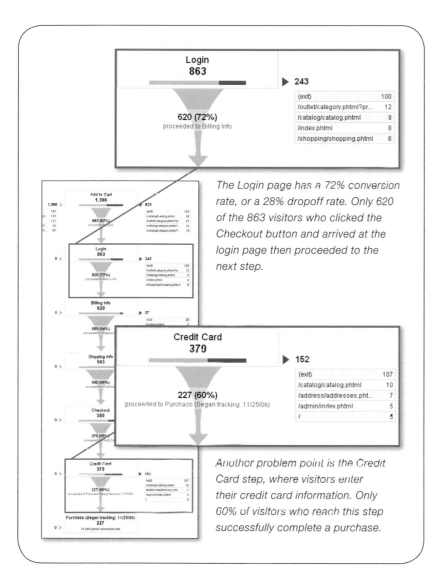

The Login page has a 72% conversion rate, or a 28% dropoff rate. Only 620 of the 863 visitors who clicked the Checkout button and arrived at the login page then proceeded to the next step.

Another problem point is the Credit Card step, where visitors enter their credit card information. Only 60% of visitors who reach this step successfully complete a purchase.

Summary

The checkout process can be hampered by visitor distrust and an outdated legacy. Pay close attention to your metrics and customize each step—your result will be a reassuring, intuitive, and efficient checkout process.

Next, we take a few pages to remind you that there is much, much more to learn than we've covered in this book, and point you to resources for further exploration and experimentation.

chapter 10

digging deeper

"Always read something that will make you look good if you die in the middle of it."

— *P.J. O'Rourke*

For those gluttons for punishment who may find themselves hooked on some of the concepts discussed herein, we've compiled a handy list of references in this chapter.

This list includes most of the references used in the book as well as a smattering of the people, writings, and research that have most influenced us in our work over the years.

This list is broken out by the following topics:

- Usability and user behavior
- Design
- Web design
- Online marketing
- Persuasion and persuasive selling
- Metrics
- Search engine marketing

What, no carrier pigeons?

After droning on for nine chapters about the importance of the web and how to get the most out of web sites, it feels strangely hypocritical to now provide a list of resources in print, where we can't even have a clickable call to action. Yet we felt the book would have been incomplete without doing so. Because we couldn't help ourselves, we've also included this list—along with an expanded set of resources on other online marketing-related topics—on our web site at www.WD4ROI.com.

We hope you'll visit us there. If you drop by, we'd love to know what you thought of the book, any results you've seen from trying some of the ideas we've discussed, or thoughts on other topics you think we should cover in future publications, should we be crazy enough to publish another book.

Usability and User Behavior

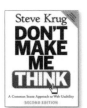

Don't Make Me Think

Steve Krug
www.sensible.com

If we had to pick one book on web usability, this would be it. We've purchased multiple copies for colleagues and clients, yet never seem to have our personal copies when we most want them because our colleagues are always stealing them. It's amazingly informative, accessible, concise, humorous, and well designed.

Designing Web Usability: *The Practice of Simplicity*

Jakob Nielsen, Ph. D.
www.nng.com

A bit more academic, this is the book that most web usability experts used in order to become web usability experts. Dr. Nielsen has been a respected usability guru, speaker, and author since before most of us were online.

Why We Buy: *The Science of Shopping Behavior*

Paco Underhill
www.envirosell.com

An entertaining and utterly fascinating look into the world of product merchandising and the psychology underlying shopper behavior.

The Humane Interface
Jef Raskin
jef.raskincenter.org

Written by the creator of the Apple Macintosh, "click-and-drag," and a few other very usable things you may have heard of, this book explores how the human mind works and ways interactive systems could be designed to be easier for humans to learn and use. Scholarly, but engaging and written with a wry humorous slant.

usability.gov

The U.S. government's web site dedicated to usability. An amazingly deep resource. While the federal government may get a bad rap for poor customer service and bureaucracy, the people behind this site are doing their part to make the online experience as intuitive as possible.

uie.com

User Interface Engineering is usability consultant, researcher, and trainer Jared Spool's company. The site is full of great information, including a very informative and entertaining blog. If you ever get the chance to see Jared Spool speak, take it. He'll make you laugh and he'll make you think—two of our favorite pastimes.

useit.com

Jakob Nielsen's site where he writes about usability. His Alertbox columns, which date back to 1995, are a treasure trove of usability information and research.

ACM SIGCHI

www.sigchi.org

This interdisciplinary special interest group focuses on the study and discussion of Computer-Human Interaction, "bringing together people working on the design, evaluation, implementation, and study of interactive computing systems for human use." There are local chapters around the world, including the active San Francisco Bay Area chapter, BayCHI.

HCI Bibliography

Human-Computer Interaction Resources
www.hcibib.org

The HCI Bibliography is a searchable gold mine of in-depth resources covering the gamut of Human-Computer Interaction topics. You'll find studies, reports, journals, and books on usability, design, and all the many ways we humans interact with computers. Of special note is the HCI humor section, proving even serious usability types have a sense of humor.

Design

Envisioning Information *(and pretty much anything else by)* Edward Tufte
www.edwardtufte.com

Edward Tufte is a master educator on information design and how design can be used to communicate even the most complex data clearly. His one-day workshop is inspiring, educational, entertaining, and may forever change the way you think about PowerPoint.

The Design of Everyday Things *(and anything else by)*

Donald Norman
www.jnd.org

Originally titled the Psychology of Everyday Things, this is a classic work on product usability by one of the leading voices on design as it relates to user experience. You'll never look at a door the same way again.

The Art of Color: *The Subjective Experience and Objective Rationale of Color*

Johannes Itten

In this classic, beautiful book on color theory, artist and educator Johannes Itten explores the use and effects of color from an artistic perspective, delving into both the objective laws and perceptual experience of color. Includes color exercises and analyses of many example paintings by great masters, old and new.

The Pantone Guide to Communicating with Color

www.pantone.com

This practical reference guide to color provides a clear insight into basic color psychology, and the effects and uses of color. Includes examples of commercial color uses and a multitude of color combination swatches to kick-start the imagination.

How to See: *A Guide to Reading Our Man-Made Environment*

George Nelson
www.dwr.com/productdetail.cfm?id=4755

Originally written by legendary artist and commercial designer George Nelson, this update is a thoughtful reminder of how disparate our own perceptions may be from those of others.

Web Design

Web Redesign 2.0: *Workflow That Works*

Kelly Goto and Emily Cotler
www.web-redesign.com

Everyone who designs and builds web sites breathed a collective sigh of relief when the first edition of this book came out in 2001. Finally someone had published a detailed methodology and explanation for how to manage web projects. Fortunately it was someone as smart and experienced as the team of Kelly Goto and Emily Cotler. If you want to learn the right process to follow for web projects, this is the book for you. Kelly is also a visionary and thought leader in the increasingly overlapping worlds of interface design, ethnography, and mobile devices. You can learn more about her work at www.gotomedia.com.

Anything by

Molly Holzschlag
www.molly.com

Renowned web guru, author, consultant, and speaker, Molly is one of the people leading the web standards movement. Visionary, strategic, and really darn smart, she's also one of the most genuine, kind, and giving people you'll ever hope to meet.

The Elements of User Experience

Jesse James Garrett
www.jjg.net

If you want to understand the underpinnings of online user experience, this book is the best. The beautiful illustrations and diagrams combine with crystal clear explanations to make this book accessible to everyone, while the concepts are engrossing even for the expert.

Online Marketing

MarketingSherpa

www.marketingsherpa.com

Publisher of the most valuable—and often
mind-blowing—articles, case studies, research,
and reports on every aspect of online market-
ing. We'd rather give up our morning coffee than our MarketingSherpa
membership. And that's saying something.

eMarketer

www.emarketer.com

The eMarketer daily newsletter is a great source
for the latest web marketing statistics. And
their full research reports are among the most
objective and insightful around.

Net Words: *Creating High-Impact Online Copy*

Nick Usborne
www.nickusborne.com

Nick Usborne is a talented copywriter, consultant, author,
and speaker. So it goes without saying that he's smart. But
he's also warm and fall-down funny. We regularly recommend him to clients who have a sense of humor.

Publish & Prosper: *Blogging for Business*

DL Byron and Steve Broback
www.texturadesign.com

Want to get up to speed on the why and how to do this
whole blogging thing right from the start? Read this book. Entrepreneur,
blogger, author, and avid cyclist DL Byron is a smart, capable guy and a
heck of a speaker.

Persuasion and Persuasive Selling

Call to Action: *Secret Formulas for Improving Online Results*

Bryan & Jeffrey Eisenberg
www.futurenowinc.com

If you want to go deeper on the topic of conversion, this is the book for you. You can also check out their very informative blog and newsletter at www.grokdotcom.com. The Eisenbergs are the godfathers of conversion marketing, yet remain surprisingly genuine and giving despite their success—and being from New York.

Persuasive Technology: *Using Computers to Change What We Think and Do*

BJ Fogg, Ph.D.
captology.stanford.edu

In this scholarly but engaging and accessible book, Dr. BJ Fogg, director of the Stanford Persuasive Technology Lab, draws from nine years of research to reveal how web sites, software applications, and mobile devices can be used to change people's attitudes and behavior. Full of scary and fascinating examples. In addition to all the other brilliant things he does, BJ also organizes the highly recommended Mobile Persuasion and Persuasive Technology conferences.

Made to Stick: *Why Some Ideas Survive and Others Die*

Chip & Dan Heath
www.madetostick.com

A refreshingly original look at what makes some concepts stick in our minds where others easily fade away. The clear framework, concrete examples, and storytelling style make for an engaging read on a fascinating topic that has surprising relevance for anyone whose job involves communicating (i.e. everyone).

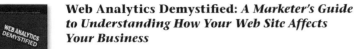

Metrics

Web Analytics Demystified: *A Marketer's Guide to Understanding How Your Web Site Affects Your Business*

Eric Peterson

An excellent guide on how to use web analytics to get the most out of your site. This book explains which metrics matter, how to interpret them, how to manage a site for continuous improvement, and more.

Web Metrics: *Proven Methods for Measuring Web Site Success*

Jim Sterne

An excellent resource for those wanting to go deeper on the topic of web metrics.

Search Engine Marketing

Search Engine Watch

www.searchenginewatch.com

The granddaddy of search engine resources, initially started by search guru Danny Sullivan. Their newsletter is excellent and their conference, Search Engine Strategies, is the biggest and best known search conference out there.

Search Engine Land

www.searchengineland.com

Danny and his colleague Chris Sherman have also created this site for more experienced search marketers. The newsletter is always insightful, as is the accompanying conference, Search Marketing Expo.

HighRankings.com

www.highrankings.com

Thousands of people have learned the ins and outs of search engine optimization from industry expert Jill Whalen. Her web site and newsletter are full of educational content, always delivered with a dose of Jill's personal warmth. If you want to learn how to optimize your site for search engines, this is a great place to start.

SEOmoz.com

www.seomoz.com

An excellent resource site for search marketers, run by the larger-than-life Rand Fishkin.

Google AdWords Handbook: *21 Ways to Maximize Results*

Andrew Goodman
www.page-zero.com/google-adwords-book.asp

Andrew Goodman is one of the smartest people in the world of pay-per-click (PPC) advertising. His Google AdWords handbook is far and away the best resource for learning how to get the most out of Google's advertising platform. Andrew's blog at www.traffick.com is also an excellent resource, full of unique insights and good humor.

Enquiro

www.enquiro.com

Both a search agency and a research firm, Enquiro and its founder Gord Hotchkiss are always on the cutting edge of the latest search marketing and user behavior trends.

Other Influences

Anything by

Guy Kawasaki
www.guykawasaki.com

Former chief evangelist at Apple and current Renaissance man Guy Kawasaki is, quite
simply, brilliant. His writing is illuminating,
irreverent and inspirational.

Getting Real: *The Smarter, Faster, Easier Way to Build a Successful Web Application*

37signals
www.37signals.com

Jason Fried and his merry band of immortals at 37signals
managed to produce this groundbreaking and engrossing
book while continuing to launch and maintain their arsenal of innovative
web-based applications now used by millions. We used their Basecamp project management tool to help us manage our book project.

Blink: *The Power of Thinking Without Thinking*

Malcolm Gladwell

What does this book have to do with the web? Plenty, it
turns out. Gladwell's clear explanations and examples of
peoples' instant reactions to various situations is the perfect
primer for understanding online user experience and why it's so important
to achieve the right first impression when someone lands on your site.

Marc Andreessen's Blog

blog.pmarca.com

As one of the co-founders of Netscape and one-time dot-com poster boy, it would be easy to forget that Marc Andreessen created the first web browser (Mosaic) as a college student and has started various other successful companies after Netscape. His wide-ranging blog is full of deep thought and rare insights.

Scott Berkun's Blog

www.scottberkun.com

An author, consultant, and software industry veteran, Scott writes with compelling humor, inspiration and insight on topics ranging from project management to usability and creative thinking. He writes some awesome books, too, including the Art of Project Management—be sure to check them out.

Piper Jaffray

www.piperjaffray.com

Piper Jaffray's research on the search and online advertising markets has been an invaluable resource for us for many years. Although our favorite analyst Safa Rashtchy has moved on, we continue to rely on their research to keep us up to speed on new developments and projections for where things are heading in this crazy online space.

The Pew Internet & American Life Project

www.pewinternet.com

An initiative of the Pew Research Center, this site provides key research reports on internet-related topics, providing information on broader U.S. trends.

Come By and Say Hello!

A more extensive list with links to all these resources and more is on our web site at www.WD4ROI.com.

We hope to see you there!

~ Lance and Sandra

index